P9-DCC-385

HOW TO CLEAN PRACTICALLY ANYTHING

FOURTH EDITION/UPDATED

HOW TO CLEAN PRACTICALLY ANYTHING

FOURTH EDITION/UPDATED

*THE EDITORS OF CONSUMER REPORTS BOOKS
WITH EDWARD KIPPEL*

Consumer Reports Books
A Division of Consumers Union
Yonkers, New York

Copyright © 1996 by Consumers Union of United States, Inc., Yonkers, New York 10703.

Published by Consumers Union of United States, Inc., Yonkers, New York 10703.

All rights reserved, including the right of reproduction in whole or in part in any form.

Library of Congress Cataloging-in-Publication Data

How to clean practically anything/the editors of Consumer Reports Books with Edward
Kippel.—4th ed./updated
   p. cm.
   Includes index
   ISBN 0-89043-843-9
   1. House Cleaning. 2. Cleaning. I. Kippel, Edward. II. Consumer Reports Books.
   TX324. H69 1996
   648.5—dc20
                                              95-37498
                                                CIP

Design by Suzette Ruys

First printing, January 1996

This book is printed on recycled paper. ♻

Manufactured in the United States of America

   How to Clean Practically Anything, Fourth Edition/Updated is a Consumer Reports
Book published by Consumers Union, the nonprofit organization that publishes
Consumer Reports, the monthly magazine of test reports, product Ratings, and buying
guidance. Established in 1936, Consumers Union is chartered under the Not-for-Profit
Corporation Law of the State of New York.

   The purposes of Consumers Union, as stated in its charter, are to provide consumers
with information and counsel on consumer goods and services, to give information on all
matters relating to the expenditure of the family income, and to initiate and to cooperate
with individual and group efforts seeking to create and maintain decent living standards.

   Consumers Union derives its income solely from the sale of *Consumer Reports* and
other publications. In addition, expenses of occasional public service efforts may be
met, in part, by nonrestrictive, noncommercial contributions, grants, and fees. Consumers Union accepts no advertising or product samples and is not beholden in any
way to any commercial interest. Its Ratings and reports are solely for the use of the
readers of its publications. Neither the Ratings, nor the reports, nor any Consumers
Union publications, including this book, may be used in advertising or for any commercial purpose. Consumers Union will take all steps open to it to prevent such uses
of its material, its name, or the name of *Consumer Reports*.

Contents

Foreword

This book contains valuable information based on Consumers Union's unbiased tests of detergents, cleaning chemicals, and cleaning equipment. In past editions, Ratings of tested products were included. But as you might imagine, these Ratings were soon out of date. So a more generic book was created, designed to be used in conjunction with recent *Consumer Reports* articles highlighting the best products for each need. If you want to find a recent report on a particular class of product, see the index in the latest issue of *Consumer Reports*, visit your local library, or contact Consumer Reports Facts by FAX at 800-766-9988. (There is a charge for each report obtained from this service.)

Acknowledgments

The editors of Consumer Reports Books would like to express their appreciation to the directors and each of the members of Consumers Union's Appliance, Chemical and Textiles, Home Environment, Public Service, and Recreation and Home Improvement departments for reviewing and providing comments designed to enhance the quality of each of the sections of this book. Among these dedicated individuals, special thanks to Edward Miller (senior project leader) and Bert Papenburg (director of testing) of the Chemical and Textiles Department for their help with many of the chapters.

Introduction

ORGANIZED CLEANING

Many people find that frequent, systematic light cleaning has advantages over periodic upheaval. For one thing, the continuous cleaning process is far easier on household surfaces. It minimizes the need for scrubbing that causes unnecessary wear and tear on wall, floor, and furniture finishes. In addition, dust on wooden surfaces, as well as on upholstery, draperies, and so forth, may be easier to remove before it builds up and combines with other soil such as body oils and tiny airborne droplets of cooking grease. Frequent vacuuming will also minimize the need for professional cleaning. Some find it easier to do a chore or two a day rather than let tasks accumulate and become overwhelming.

PLANNING

Develop a list of all tasks that need to be done during the year and group them under frequency headings—daily, weekly, monthly, semiannually, and annually. It may be possible to budget your time so that weekly chores are spread out over several days. For people with weekday responsibilities other than cleaning, house

1

maintenance must be on a catch-as-catch-can basis. But even within the limits of available time, it's a good idea to plan to accomplish household tasks on a regular schedule.

What you clean and how often you clean depend upon your personal preferences and tolerances. The following schedule is meant as a guideline to suggest how a home can be cleaned with well-defined tasks. Divide responsibilities among all family members. Make certain that everyone knows who does what and when.

Daily. Dishes should be washed, dried, and put away, and kitchen counters wiped after each meal. Clean the kitchen sink and wipe the range surfaces (including the microwave oven) once a day or, even better, after each use. Picking up should become second nature.

Weekly. Dust furniture and shelves; vacuum and, where applicable, brush upholstered furniture. Vacuum rugs and floors. Clean under furniture and behind it. Damp mop the kitchen floor. Empty wastebaskets. Wash bathroom basins, fixtures, and floors. Dust radiators, woodwork, pictures, and mirrors. Wipe window sills, and brush shades and blinds. Clean kitchen range burners. Wipe the refrigerator and kitchen cabinet fronts. Polish bright metal surfaces.

Monthly. Do one or more of the following special jobs in several rooms on the same day: vacuum and, where applicable, brush curtains and draperies. Wipe wood trim and, where needed, wipe walls and around doorknobs. Wash windows. Wash and, if necessary, wax the kitchen floor. Polish wood furniture and vacuum upholstered furniture, paying special attention to cleaning under cushions and in crevices between the back and the cushion support. To prolong their life, turn over mattresses, end to end and side to side, which will help equalize their wear. In hot weather, clean air conditioner filters according to the manufacturer's recommendations.

Seasonally or semiannually. Take inventory of the items in closets and drawers that are no longer useful. (The more clutter, the harder it is to clean.) Rearrange clothes closets by season, hanging clothes by type for easy access. Weed out unused clothing that can be donated to appropriate agencies. Pack winter and summer clothing where it will remain clean and free from moth damage until needed again. (Dry-cleaning establishments commonly offer free storage for items you bring them for cleaning.) Pack wool clothing in cloth bags. This will allow the fiber to breathe and prevent moth damage. Wash mattress covers. Wash curtains and draperies or have them dry cleaned. Dust the coils behind or underneath the refrigerator.

Annually. Have the furnace cleaned and tuned in late spring or early fall. A central air-conditioning system and room air conditioners should be checked for proper operation before the onset of hot weather. Put power and hand gardening tools in good order—cleaned, oiled, and greased—before storing them for the winter. The same applies to snow removal equipment in the spring. Shampoo carpets and rugs or have them cleaned professionally every 12 to 18 months.

EQUIPMENT AND STORAGE

If everything is kept organized, it will be easier for you to work and you won't waste time looking for something when you need it. If you live in a two- or three-story dwelling, it might be worth the investment to duplicate supplies—such as vacuum cleaners—so that you can have them on the same floor where they are used. Keep special bathroom cleaning equipment and supplies in or near the bathroom, if space permits.

Keep cleaning equipment as clean and dry as possible, so that it's ready for the next use. Be sure that any enclosure where cleaning materials are stored has ventilation holes in the door to allow volatile materials to evaporate from cloths, sponges, and mops. Brooms and brushes should not rest on their bristles. Hang them to prevent premature wear and deformation that result in loss of usefulness. Since cleaning products are often hazardous, make sure the shelves on which they are stored are high enough to be out of reach of young children.

Avoid cluttering a cleaning closet with rarely used supplies and equipment. Keep a supply of paper vacuum-cleaner dust bags on hand. Use the brand that is recommended for your particular vacuum; off-brand bags may not work well. You may also want to stock spare sponge-mop refills, as well as a package or two of hand sponges.

Good dust cloths can be made from cast-off soft cotton garments and bedding. Although they may be costlier to use—and some might be less effective than cloth and harsh on some surfaces—some people find paper towels convenient. Cloths will hold dust better if they are pretreated. A simple method is to put a cloth into a screw-cap glass jar that has been coated on the inside with furniture polish. Put about two teaspoons of liquid polish into a container and turn it until a thin layer of polish covers the inside surface. Let the cloth stand in the jar for a day or two.

ANOTHER SOLUTION

Housecleaning takes time and effort. One obvious way to escape cleaning, although the solution can be expensive, is to employ a qualified, reliable, and courteous home-cleaning service. Some people use a professional service once or twice a year; others employ a cleaning person once a week or every two weeks or so. If you decide to use professional help, ask for referrals from reliable neighbors and friends. If that fails, check the Yellow Pages under Housecleaning. Always ask for and check references.

When negotiating with a prospective housecleaning provider, be sure you both understand what is going to be done, how long it will take, how much it will cost, and how frequently and on what day of the week they'll provide the service. Be sure there is an understanding of what cleaning materials and equipment they'll bring and what you will have to make available. Tell them where the items you're responsible for will be kept. Be sure the cleaning provider regularly tells you when supplies are low so you can stock up before their next visit.

HELPFUL HINTS

Few of us like to clean, but it is something we have to do, so why not minimize the effort required. The following suggestions should make the task of cleaning easier.

■ It is not necessary to clean things that are not dirty. Sometimes, all that is needed is a touch-up. You do not need to dry-clean a suit when it only has to be aired, brushed, or pressed. If there is a hand print on an otherwise perfectly clean mirror, don't feel you have to clean the whole mirror; just attack the print.
■ If you don't need or like something in your house, give it away, dispose of it, or recycle it rather than having to clean it.
■ Always clean from top to bottom. (Gravity carries dust down onto lower surfaces.)
■ Surfaces that you or your visitors can't see—like the top of a cabinet—don't have to be cleaned regularly. Put some paper down, and when it gets too dirty, pick the paper up and throw it out.

■ If you're vacuuming in a large room, add a 25- to 50-foot extension cord to avoid the exasperation of having to stop and relocate the plug. Be sure the cord has the same power rating as the vacuum.

■ Place mats strategically at each entrance to collect dirt that would otherwise be tracked in from the outside onto carpets and floors. Encourage friends and family to wipe their feet before entering the house.

■ Avoid any more walking back and forth than is absolutely necessary by gathering all the supplies you'll need for a particular project and bringing them along with you at one time in a pail-style organizer.

■ Before using any new cleaning product or an old-standby product on a new item, be sure to spot-test it on an inconspicuous part of the item for possible damage. Pretesting for possible damage is especially important. It will be mentioned often throughout this book.

■ Store all household cleaning products in their original containers, with original labels intact so you'll be able to refresh your memory with regard to directions for use, suggested precautions, and possible antidotes. Before using any new cleaning product, be sure to read the product's label carefully. Product formulations can change, so it is also prudent to read the labels on your old standby products before using a new container.

■ To replace a foam cushion taken from a zippered cover, place the cushion in a plastic garbage bag and insert the bag open-end first into the cover. Then, all you have to do is pull the bag out, leaving the foam in place.

■ Be careful when cleaning windows to avoid getting window cleaner on adjacent painted surfaces, furniture, or carpeting and damaging them.

■ Don't buy furnishings solely with aesthetics in mind. When purchasing a carpet or piece of furniture, be sure to ask about issues related to maintenance. Look for cleanability codes on upholstered furniture. An "X" code means the piece cannot be cleaned by any method other than vacuuming.

■ Maximize lighting when cleaning or attempting to remove a stain. That way you won't miss an important area that requires your attention.

■ If you plan to have your carpets or furniture cleaned professionally, be sure to remove pets and plants that might be affected by cleaning chemicals. Keep family members and pets out until everything is dry and you are given the "all clear" to enter the area.

Dishes

DISHWASHER DETERGENTS

"Liquid gel" detergents solve the two major drawbacks of liquid dishwasher detergents: the liquids tend to dribble out of the dishwasher's main wash cup yet tend to empty incompletely from their containers, leaving a sizable amount unused. The gels are free-flowing and dispense completely from their containers.

The gels are better than powders at removing lipstick from glasses and cups. But the powders are better than gels in overall dishwashing, cleaning dried-on foods, and preventing washed off foods from spotting and resoiling dishes.

While all the dishwasher detergents Consumers Union has tested tend to discolor silver-plated flatware, after long exposure powders tend to be slightly safer than gels in this regard. Powders and gels both etch glassware when used in soft water. Typically, damage to glassware is less likely in hard water. Powders and most gels are safer to use on fine china with overglaze patterns than they used to be years ago. However, it would be prudent to hand wash fine china, silver, and crystal.

COSTS

Store brands tend to be the cheaper products to use. Two powders not sold in stores—*Shaklee Basic-D Concentrate* and *Amway Crystal Bright*—deserve special mention because of their extraordinarily high price and cost per load. Although both are excellent in overall dishwashing, so are other, much-less-expensive powders.

ENVIRONMENTAL EFFECTS

Most dishwasher detergents contain phosphates. Phosphates help dishwasher detergents do their job better, especially in hard water. Over the years, manufacturers have worked on reducing the amount of phosphates in dishwasher detergents, and a few have been able to eliminate them altogether. But dishwasher detergents with phosphates are still permitted everywhere.

RINSE AGENTS

In areas of the country with hard water, there is a more pronounced tendency for spots or film to form on glassware and dishes after a wash. If your dishwasher leaves spots or film, change your brand of detergent or try a rinse agent. A rinse agent is designed to lower the surface tension of water, causing it to sheet off the dishes. This helps the dishwasher rinse away spots and film.

DISHWASHERS

Most dishwashers offer some variation on the basic wash-rinse-dry cycle. A dishwasher's Normal or Regular cycle typically includes two washes interspersed with two or three rinses. A Heavy cycle can entail longer wash periods, a third wash, hotter water, or all of the above. A Light cycle usually includes just one wash.

These basic cycles are probably all that is needed. Additional washing and drying options abound, necessary or not.

The common Rinse and Hold option can be useful for small families. Instead of stacking dirty dishes in the sink or the dishwasher, you can gradually accumulate a full load, rinsing the dishes as you go.

Don't expect a machine that offers a Pots and Pans cycle to do the work that requires abrasive cleaners and elbow grease. And think twice before subjecting good crystal or china—especially sets with gold trim—to a dishwasher's China/Crystal setting. The harsh detergents and possible jostling could etch or otherwise damage fine china.

WASHING AND DRYING

Fancy electronic controls don't necessarily translate into better cleaning. Most machines, electronic or not, work pretty well overall. Most machines also use their water-heating element to dry the dishes; some have a blower or a separate duct-mounted heater. Whatever the method, your machine should do an excellent job of drying china and glasses. Drying flatware is a bit more demanding for some.

No-heat air drying, which utilizes evaporation and heat retained from the wash, produces reasonably dry dishes provided you can wait a few hours. You may be able to speed up drying by propping open the door.

ENERGY AND NOISE

If you don't rinse dishes before you load—and you needn't—a dishwasher actually uses no more water than hand washing with a double sink. In fact, a dishwasher uses less water than if you washed dishes under a running faucet. The machines themselves use a small amount of electricity, consuming between 0.6 and 1.4 kilowatt-hours of electricity when supplied with 120°F water, which works out to between 5 and 12 cents of electricity at average power rates. No-heat drying saves a penny or two.

Heating water to feed the dishwasher accounts for the bulk of its energy costs. An electric water heater will consume about 12 cents of electricity to provide the 9 gallons of 120°F water typically used for one load; the total comes to about $45 a year, assuming you run the dishwasher once a day. The hot-water cost for a gas- or oil-fired heater will be about 4 cents a load, or a total of about $15 a year.

Quiet operation has become a dishwasher's main selling point, second only to washing performance and durability. Dishwashers have become quieter over the years.

SAFETY

All models have a safety interlock that will turn off the power when the door is opened. All models have a float switch, which senses accidental overfilling and also cuts power.

Many dishwasher accidents involve people cutting themselves, usually on knives or forks as they reach over a flatware basket into the machine's dish rack. It's always a good idea to load flatware with their points down. In addition, a machine's heating element can inflict a serious burn. Make sure that the appliance has cooled before you reach into the bottom of the tub to clean a filter or retrieve an item that has dropped.

Door vents, often at a toddler's eye level, can emit steam, so keep children away while the dishwasher is running. Some electronic models have a hidden touchpad that locks the controls to discourage children from playing with them—a worthwhile feature.

DISHWASHER RELIABILITY

Some of the more reliable brands, based on the experiences of *Consumer Reports* readers with dishwashers bought new since 1987, have been Magic Chef, Whirlpool, Hotpoint, Amana, General Electric Monogram, and General Electric. Frigidaire, Tappan, and White-Westinghouse dishwashers were most frequently reported as having needed repairs.

HAND DISHWASHING LIQUIDS

Hand dishwashing liquids are formulated to facilitate removal of greasy soil from dishes (glasses, plates, utensils, pots, etc.). They also suspend (emulsify) the soil in the wash water to facilitate rinsing. Although a hand dishwashing liquid does not have to produce any meaningful amount of suds to be effective at removing soil, suds stability has become accepted (rightly or wrongly) as an indication of a product's remaining cleaning power.

Consumers Union surveyed staff members regarding their dishwashing habits. The respondents reported using one or more of the following methods. In fact, many of the respondents reported using all three methods.

- Squirt a quantity of hand dishwashing liquid into a sink, dishpan, or equivalent before or during the process of filling it with water. Then clean the dishes using a sponge, brush, plastic scrubbing pad, or dishcloth.
- Squirt some detergent into the dish and wash it using a sponge, brush, plastic scrubbing pad, or dishcloth.
- Squirt some detergent directly onto a sponge, brush, plastic scrubbing pad, or dishcloth, which is then used to wash the dishes.

THE PRODUCTS

Most products have pull-up dispensing tops. Some have snap-top dispensing caps or screw caps without dispensers. The 22-fluid-ounce size is commonly used. However, many products come in larger sizes, and ultraconcentrated versions come in smaller containers. Most containers have contoured shapes, presumably for ease of gripping.

Hand dishwashing liquids may contain alcohol to keep the surfactants dissolved; alcohol may irritate some individuals' hands. They may also contain fragrances, preservatives, and colorants, which can also irritate.

PRODUCT PERFORMANCE

Most test methods for hand dishwashing liquids are based *entirely* on the products' ability to sustain a head of foam in hard water while challenged by soiled plates. The number of plates that hand dishwashing liquids will wash before the suds are depleted varies from product to product and is affected by water hardness. In Consumers Union testing, several well-known national brands washed more than 12 plates in both hard and soft water. Most of the brands will not do much worse.

But suds stability is not the most important characteristic of good hand dishwashing liquids. Their primary function is to facilitate the removal of greasy soil. Hand dishwashing liquids do not remove soil by themselves, especially carbonized (burned on) food residues (e.g., the fat in a broiler pan), which can be difficult. They help loosen and emulsify the soil so you can *more easily* remove it with some amount of elbow grease and the help of a dish cloth, sponge, steel wool, or plastic scrubbing pad.

Typically, the hand dishwashing liquids Consumers Union tested were more effective at removing greasy soil in hard water than in soft water. They were very good to excellent in hard water, whereas the best products were only very good in soft water. (Most were merely good.) However, some were not much better than using only hot water—which is not very good at all.

In hard water, the better products (especially the ones with the best suds stability) might be slightly more difficult to rinse than most of the others. In soft water the differences are less significant.

Many Consumers Union staff members reported that they never use protective gloves when they clean dishes, whereas 22 percent use them some of the time. Although most of those who never wear gloves or wear them only some of the time reported that they had not experienced any skin irritation, about 20 percent had.

Contrary to claims that some products attack grease but not skin oils, the surfactants in all hand dishwashing liquids will remove natural oils from the skin. Accordingly, none of these products will actually be beneficial for your hands. But some products are less harsh than others. Consumers Union found the best "natural" brands to be almost as mild as baby shampoo. Whereas most products tested were at least as mild as an adult shampoo, a few might be more irritating to some people's hands.

DOSE

Very few products provide the user with any definitive dose information. In fact, several tell the user to employ "one firm squeeze." To see what a "squeeze" might deliver, Consumers Union staff members were asked to show how much hand dishwashing liquid they would squeeze into a sink or dishpan. The results varied from less than 1 gram to about 25 grams. Thus, instructions to use a "firm squeeze" to dispense hand dishwashing liquid do not provide enough information for proper dose control.

RECOMMENDATIONS

If you normally use a hand dishwashing liquid to clean a few lightly soiled dishes like milk or soft drink glasses, soup bowls or sandwich plates, it may be best to apply a few drops of the product to a dishcloth or sponge and refresh it as needed. However, if you wash a sink full of dishes, start with a dilute solution (about one tablespoon of hand dishwashing liquid for every three to four gallons of water). If this does not do an adequate cleaning job, add more. To clean heavily soiled pots, pans, and dishes, you'll need a product with the ability to effectively emulsify the grease and loosen the tough soil, thereby making the scrubbing job as easy as possible.

No matter which product you choose, use water that is as hot as your hands can bear. Rubber gloves will permit use of the hottest possible water; they'll also protect sensitive hands from irritation. The hot water will help to soften the greasy soil, making it easier for the hand dishwashing liquid's surfactants to loosen and emulsify it. When washing in a dishpan or sink, wash dishes and utensils by groups. Start with the least soiled group and end with those having the heaviest soil build-up. A good sequence is glasses, flatware, plates, serving dishes, and pots/pans last.

OTHER USES

Hand dishwashing liquids are very versatile. They can be used to clean dirty hands, they can be used to hand launder delicate washable clothing, and, as mentioned throughout this book, they can be used for many other stain removal and cleaning purposes.

Caution: Do not use a hand dishwashing liquid in an automatic dishwasher—it will oversuds.

Floors

CARPET AND RUG CLEANING

Typical supermarket carpet-cleaning products include powders, foam shampoos that come in a pressurized can, and liquids sprayed straight from the container. A few concentrated products—powder or liquid—must be mixed with water.

Most manufacturers recommend that you gently work the cleaner into the carpet with a brush and remove the residue with a regular vacuum cleaner (liquids, of course, need time to dry first).

Manual carpet cleaning isn't as unpleasant as it might sound. The powders minimize the mess, and the job goes quickly. The powders are almost dry, so the room can be used immediately afterward. (Actually, "dry" powders are slightly moist.)

Stains are likely to be a problem for supermarket carpet-cleaning products. None of the ones tested in the past were better than fair in treating any of Consumers Union's test stains.

CLEANING WITH A MACHINE

Wet-cleaning machines (also known as "steamers" or hot-water extraction equipment) are usually sold or rented with a recommended cleaning product. The majority of machines use a hot detergent solution, which the machine sprays on the rug. They not only apply the solution but also use suction to remove it. The need for water complicates matters. Some machines get their water supply via a long hose that you attach to a hot-water faucet. As you clean, the hose is dragged along. In other models, you fill a reservoir with hot water. With both kinds, you will eventually need to pour out the dirty water, which is collected either in the base of the machine or in a removable container. When full, the part you empty can weigh almost 50 pounds.

With any machine that uses water, or with any wet cleaner you scrub yourself, you must wait for the carpet to dry before walking

GUIDELINES FOR DO-IT-YOURSELF CARPET CLEANING

Be sure to give your carpet a thorough vacuuming before you start the wet cleaning process. Whether you use a rented "steamer" or one purchased for regular use, read the manufacturer's instructions carefully before attempting to shampoo your carpet.

Use an extra "dry stroke." A carpet's cleanliness can be optimized by ensuring that your machine provides good extraction. Make an extraction pass with the water spray on, then make a second pass with the water spray off. This increases the amount of water removed from the carpeting. Check your work by wiping your hand across the top of the carpeting. If you get drops of water, extract the carpeting again with the spray off. If your hand is damp and the carpet feels like a wrung-out sponge, you are extracting correctly.

Use the correct chemicals. Use *only* chemicals designed to clean carpeting, and use them according to the manufacturer's recommended concentrations. If the package says to use one ounce, measure it out. Be sure you do not use too much. *Do not* use laun-

on it, which can take at least overnight. There's also a risk of wetting the carpet too much. Water can seep through and damage a hardwood floor or the latex backing of an old carpet (it shouldn't hurt the polyolefin backing of most new carpets but can delaminate adhesives).

Rented wet-cleaning machines are likely to be larger than those sold to homeowners. This can pose transportation problems if you don't have access to a vehicle with adequate cargo space.

Instead of water and detergent, some machines use powder. They may apply the powder, work it in, and use suction to remove

---

dry soap, shampoo, dish soap, etc., to clean your carpet. Never put any kind of bleach through the extraction equipment. Bleach can ruin your carpet and void a manufacturer's warranty. You can usually find carpet-cleaning chemicals close to carpet-cleaning rental equipment or in the cleaning section of a grocery store. Some of the major brands of carpet-cleaning chemicals have been tested by major fiber producers and approved for use on stain-resistant carpeting.

Pre-spray where necessary. If your carpeting is "really dirty," increase the amount of pre-spray (often called traffic lane cleaner) that you use. Do not increase the amount of carpet detergent.

Neutralize. A final vinegar-water rinse (1 cup of white vinegar in 1 gallon of plain water) and a thorough extraction are helpful to remove and neutralize any detergent residue in the carpet.

Dry properly. Allow the carpet to dry completely. Open windows and move air through the house with fans. Keep family members and pets off the carpet until it is dry.

it, or they may merely apply the powder and provide agitation. You then use your own vacuum cleaner to clean it up. It is important to vacuum thoroughly to prevent powder buildup. Residual powder may cause problems if you wet-clean your carpet at a later date. If your household vacuum will not do an adequate job, consider renting a commercial vacuum. (Before using a powder rug cleaner, be sure to read your vacuum cleaner owner's manual for possible precautions regarding these materials.) Follow the manufacturer's recommendations regarding the length of time to leave the powder on the carpet.

PROFESSIONAL CLEANING

Carpets. Ideally, a professional cleaning service should visit your home to carefully evaluate the carpet's condition before rendering an estimate, but often this does not happen. Some cleaning services will provide a preliminary price pending closer inspection in the home. This is perfectly acceptable if the cleaners do a careful inspection and requote (if necessary) before cleaning begins.

The cleaning service should discuss its procedures in detail. Depending on the carpet's condition, it may not be possible to clean the carpet completely. The company should inform the customer if its cleaners will not be able to remove a stain without damage. There shouldn't be any surprises.

Ask the company what it will do if its cleaners damage the carpet, and ascertain how they will protect adjacent furniture. Be sure to check references to determine if the cleaning service adheres to these precautions during the job.

Rugs. Loose rugs, especially handmade ones, should be removed and cleaned professionally "in-plant" rather than in your home. Rug cleaners offer extra services such as repairing the fringe, reweaving, and moth-resistant treatment.

You can take any size rug to a professional cleaner or, for an extra fee, some cleaning companies will pick up and drop off a rug. If you call a service that comes to your home, try to arrange a definite appointment, or you might have to wait at home all day.

RECOMMENDATIONS

Carpet manufacturers recommend cleaning household carpet every 6 to 18 months, depending on the level of traffic. To maximize the time between cleanings, keep dirt outside with mats at each entry.

Whether you do the work yourself or hire professionals, be sure to clean your carpet regularly to prevent buildup of soil. Many do-it-yourself products should be able to handle a lightly soiled carpet. Ground-in dirt and stains from spills are much more difficult to remove. In general, when a rug has been soiled by garden-variety dirt, it's better to send it out to professionals or to call in a professional cleaning service.

First Aid for Carpet Stains

Although no carpet is completely stain proof, most modern carpets have been treated to render them stain resistant. If you act quickly, most spills can be removed easily. A delay in taking action will increase the probability of the stain's becoming permanent. With some spilled substances—children's fruit drinks, for instance—you have only minutes before the stain sets permanently.

Do not scrub the stained area. Doing so can cause pile distortion. Wherever possible, immediately blot up spills using a *clean white* absorbent material to avoid the possibility of dye transfer and to facilitate inspection of the stain removal process while stains transfer to the towel. When the stain has been removed, continue to blot with dry cloths or paper towels until the area is completely dry.

If the spill remains on the carpet for a long time and becomes a dry mass, scrape off as much as possible using the side of a spoon or a *blunt* spatula before attempting to remove the remainder. For chewing gum or wax, freeze with an ice cube before scraping. Be sure to vacuum up all remaining solid residue.

If the cause of a spot can be identified, it may be possible to remove it yourself. Refer to Appendix B: Stain Removal, and carefully adhere to the recommended directions.

Copious spills that penetrate through the carpet to the backing and even to the floor are a special problem. If the substance smells, the carpet may have to be lifted and cleaned. Consider hiring professional carpet cleaners rather than attempting to do the job yourself. Just blot it up and get help. (Do-it-yourself cleaning efforts might render the stain difficult for even an expert to remove.)

Household products that contain bleach, hydrogen peroxide, or some other oxidizing agent can cause irreversible damage. A leaking container of laundry bleach is an obvious villain. Other products are more insidious. The damage caused by acne, foot, or dog mange medications containing benzoyl peroxide, for instance, often doesn't show up right away. Those medications, typically hard to wash off, have ruined many a carpet. Benzoyl peroxide is activated by moisture from humidity, a spilled drink, or wet cleaning of carpets. Impossible-to-remove discolorations may show up after contact with moisture. Other products to watch out for include swimming pool chemicals, drain cleaners, toilet bowl cleaners, mildew removers, liquid plant foods, and pesticides.

FLOOR CARE

Vinyl is one of the most widely used man-made flooring materials. It is available in conventional and no-wax styles. For durability, choose a thick vinyl with homogeneous color that extends through the entire thickness. The no-wax versions have a clear wear-layer on the surface. Other man-made flooring materials include linoleum (which is highly susceptible to damage from strong cleaners), asphalt tile (which is hard but brittle), and rubber tile (a very quiet flooring material). Natural flooring materials include wood, cork, masonry, stone, marble, terrazzo, ceramic tile, quarry tile, terra cotta, slate, and concrete.

The basic rule for proper floor care is to pick the right product for the job. There are three basic categories of floor care products: products that clean, combination products that both clean and shine, and products that add a protective shine to the floor.

FLOOR CLEANERS

Floor cleaners remove dirt and soil from resilient floors or well-sealed wood floors. Some can leave a dulling residue that must be washed away. For no-wax flooring, be sure to use a product that is formulated for that purpose.

COMBINATION PRODUCTS

These products combine cleaning agents for dirt removal and polishing agents that add protection and shine. Since there are many types of combination floor care products, be sure to read the label recommendations pertaining to the types of flooring they claim to be good for. Some combination products are self-removing, whereas others should be removed periodically. If you have no-wax flooring, you may not need to use a combination product, even for cleaning. If you have very shiny, polyurethane-finished wood floors, polish won't make any real difference in appearance. But on no-wax vinyl-surfaced floors, whose shine is a bit less glaring, polish can add a touch of gloss.

If you have a vinyl no-wax floor and feel compelled to use polish, you won't be doing anything but boosting the shine. The amount of protection offered by a thin film of polish is insignificant compared with the protection offered by the vinyl flooring itself.

Even rugged plastics such as polyurethane and vinyl can get scratched and worn over time. It is also reasonable to assume that an accumulation of tiny scratches will eventually dull no-wax flooring a little. The polishes in combination floor cleaners may have some ability to fill in tiny scratches, which might improve the shine of worn areas. Until a no-wax floor is worn, however, floor polish is a waste of money. You'd be better off saving that money to make up for the extra cost of the no-wax flooring.

WAXING FLOORS THAT NEED IT

Before deciding to wax a no-wax floor that looks dull, attempt to remove any residue buildup that might be causing the dull look. Use a no-rinse floor cleaner and scrub the floor with a mop or stiff bristle brush, wiping up the loosened soil as you clean. You may need to clean the floor three or four times to completely remove the residue. Once the floor is free of residue, use a floor polish that is formulated for no-wax floors to renew the shine.

Conventional floor polishes are used to protect and add or restore shine to resilient floors, as well as stone or masonry floors. They are applied after the floor has been cleaned, rinsed, and dried. They dry shiny and require periodic removal.

REMOVING OLD WAX

Technology has produced polishes that don't need buffing, but it has been less successful in eliminating the chore of stripping off old polish as the layers build up. Even polishes labeled as self-cleaning leave a small amount of old polish behind. The problem is usually most noticeable in corners, where the polish isn't worn away by traffic. While you may be content to let the layers of wax accumulate for a long time before trying to remove them, it is best to remove old polish after six or eight coats, or at least once a year.

The typical recipe for removing old floor wax is ½ cup of powdered floor cleaner and 2 cups of ammonia in 1 gallon of cool water, some fine steel wool, and a lot of elbow grease. There are also wax removers on the market. Some are recommended on the labels of their brand-mate floor polishes.

RECOMMENDATIONS

It is important to have a regular floor-care schedule. Floors that are heavily trafficked will require more frequent maintenance than floors that get less use. Spills are more noticeable on very light and very dark floors. Solid-colored floors show soil more quickly than patterned floors.

Blot spills up as soon as they occur. Do not rub—it could cause a dull spot. This is especially true for polished floors.

Remove dirt regularly from wood and cork floors using a broom, lightweight vacuum cleaner, or dust mop. Small particles can scratch the flooring. Periodically restore the shine by rebuffing or using a wax that removes the previous layer as the new layer is applied. Stubborn spots can be removed by rubbing with fine steel wool or, preferably, a plastic mesh sponge dipped in a solvent-based wax.

Washable floors should first be cleaned with a broom, dust mop, or vacuum cleaner. They should then be damp mopped using water and an all-purpose cleaner recommended for washing floors. Wring out the mop before using it, and change the cleaning solution as often as possible.

For taking care of new or fairly new no-wax floors, use a plain damp mop or a little detergent followed by a rinse. When the floor is so worn that it looks as if it really needs a polish, choose among the no-wax floor cleaning products or use a combination product that is recommended for use on no-wax floors. Take particular care to rinse off combination cleaners after each use.

HARD-SURFACE-FLOOR FIRST AID FOR STAINS

When using any household chemicals, handle them with care and store them out of the reach of children. Never mix chemicals with each other or with household cleaning products unless there are specific directions to do so. Wear rubber gloves when working with alcohol, hydrogen peroxide solution, household ammonia, acids, or chlorine bleach. To be on the safe side, it's a good idea to work in a well-ventilated room: Establish cross ventilation with open windows and doors and a window fan to exhaust air.

Caution: Never mix ammonia and chlorine
bleach.

Before using any chemical, test it on a small corner of the stain. If your procedure is wrong, the chemical damage will be limited to that one area. If you use steel wool on a stain, use grade 00 and rub gently. On wood, rub with the grain.

After you have tried ordinary hand dishwashing liquid and water applied with a rag or sponge—or a nonbleaching all-purpose liquid cleaner sprayed from its container—try these suggestions to remove a variety of potentially stubborn stains. Whenever possible, work on a wet stain before it has had a chance to soak in and/or dry.

Alcoholic beverages. Try rubbing with a clean cloth dampened with rubbing alcohol.

Blood. Try clear, cold water first (before any detergent). If the stain remains, cautiously apply a solution of ammonia and cold water, and quickly rinse to avoid discoloration.

Candle wax or chewing gum. Use ice cubes to chill the material to brittleness. Then, using a plastic spatula, carefully scrape the wax or gum from the floor.

Cigarette burn. For heavy stains, try scouring powder and a piece of fine steel wool or a plastic scouring pad dipped in water. For hard-surface floors, rub with a cloth dampened with a solution of lemon juice and water.

Coffee or fruit juice. Saturate a cloth with a solution of one part glycerine to three parts water and place it over the stain for several hours. (Glycerine is available in drugstores.) If the spot remains, rub it gently with scouring powder and a cloth dampened in hot water.

Dyes. After applying on an inconspicuous spot to be sure the floor will not be damaged, rub with a cloth dampened in a solution of one part chlorine bleach and two parts water. If this doesn't work, try scouring powder and a cloth dampened with hot water.

Grease and oil. Remove as much as possible with newspaper, paper towels, or a plastic spatula. On resilient tile, rub with a cloth dampened in hand dishwashing liquid and warm water (or an all-purpose cleaner). On wood and cork, place a cloth saturated with dry cleaning fluid on the stain for no more than 5 minutes. Then wipe the area dry and wash with detergent and water.

Ink. Try a commercial ink remover, carefully following instructions, or use rubbing alcohol. It might be helpful to cover the stain with a poultice of diatomaceous earth and alcohol, cover with plastic wrap, and let stand overnight.

Lipstick. Try fine steel wool wet with detergent and water. If the floor is hard surfaced or has a no-wax finish, or is embossed vinyl composition, use a plastic scouring pad instead of steel wool.

Mustard. Place a cloth soaked in hydrogen peroxide solution over the stain. Over that, place an ammonia-soaked cloth. Leave in place until the stain has faded, sponge with water, and wipe open your blinds or curtains for one to two days. The sunlight may fade residual mustard stains.

Paint or varnish. On resilient tile, use liquid or all-purpose detergent with either a cloth, a sponge, or fine steel wool very carefully applied. On a hard-surface floor, scrub with a concentrated solution of powdered detergent and water, or apply undiluted liquid laundry detergent.

Rust. Use a commercial rust remover intended for your particular type of floor.

Shoe polish or nail polish. If concentrated detergent solution doesn't work on resilient flooring, try scouring powder or steel wool. On wood and cork, fine steel wool should do the trick. Don't use nail polish remover; it may soften resilient flooring.

Tar. Use ice cubes to chill the tar to brittleness. Then scrape the tar carefully with a plastic spatula. To remove the tar stain, apply a damp cloth wrapped around a paste made of powdered detergent, chalk, or diatomaceous earth, and water. Leave the paste on the stain for several hours.

Urine. After applying on an inconspicuous spot to be sure the floor will not be damaged, rub with a hot, damp cloth and scouring powder. For increased effectiveness, place a cloth soaked in hydrogen peroxide over the stain and cover that with a cloth soaked in ammonia. Leave in place until the stain has faded, sponge with water, and wipe dry.

FINISHING TOUCHES

After you have successfully removed a stain, refinishing may be necessary. Rinse the area well and allow it to dry before you apply any new finish (polish, for example). The newly finished area should blend in with the rest of the floor within a day or two.

Furniture

WOOD FURNITURE

Some say keeping wood furniture clean should require a minimum amount of care, asserting that the oil or lacquer finish normally used on furniture protects the wood (by sealing). Others believe that the original finish itself needs a protective layer—usually a wax—that should be renewed periodically. Between those who opt for no wax and those who recommend lots of wax are those who say you should use a little wax sometimes.

At one time, a key part of spring cleaning involved giving the furniture a fresh coat of wax—paste wax, no less, applied with plenty of muscle. The wax was supposed to "feed" the wood and help protect it. No doubt, some people still hew to that ritual.

Consumers Union's testers have found that, in general, the need for waxing and cleaning furniture with a brand-name product is often quite unnecessary. Most furniture won't benefit from waxing because its surface has been sealed at the factory with a durable finish that keeps the wood from drying out and, to some degree, protects against spills and minor scratches. Oils and waxes don't penetrate the finish. The minuscule residue that remains from most polishes after application and buffing contributes nothing to damage control.

Modern furniture does need cleaning, however. Dust, smoke, and greasy cooking fumes combine to create a dulling film. Fingerprints begin as small smudges and grow to a grimy coating.

You can choose among dozens of furniture cleaners at the supermarket. Many, like the familiar *Pledge, Behold,* and *Endust,* are intended primarily to help remove dust. Others, such as *Kleen 'n Shine* and *Murphy's Oil Soap,* are intended for cleaning wood and other surfaces. Hardware stores carry still other furniture cleaners and polishes, generally oil-based products such as *Old English Red Oil* and *Scott's Liquid Gold.* Only a few actually contain wax.

Except for old furniture whose original finish may not have sealed the wood very well—or newer furniture that has been used a lot and whose finish may be worn thin—regular dusting with a soft rag slightly dampened with water may be all you need to keep furniture looking new and clean. It's still true, however, that finely finished wood and wood with a modern, well-sealed finish should be treated with respect when it comes to water. A wood furniture cleaner should first be tested on an inconspicuous area before attempting any cleaning or treatment method. Be sure

---

HOME BREWS

In addition to plain water and dishwashing liquid, Consumers Union found the following home brews did a creditable cleaning job on wood furniture:

- ■ ½ teaspoon light olive oil added to ¼ cup white vinegar. This proved to be as effective as any store product.
- ■ ¼ cup walnut oil plus 4 drops of lemon extract. This was only as effective as the better oil-based products.

---

to read product labels carefully, paying particular attention to prohibited actions.

The mirror finish on a piece of wood furniture is there courtesy of the furniture maker. The shine you get from a product depends almost entirely on the nature of the furniture's original finish. For instance, no polish is likely to increase the luster of a piano top made from high-gloss mahogany. It is already mirrorlike. Furthermore, the finish isn't likely to be protected to any degree by using furniture polish.

Waxing won't improve the shine of furniture whose original finish is still intact. In fact, a furniture polish may muddy the finish. A buildup of wax can darken the wood and mask its grain. Some oils (such as lemon oil) applied to a previously waxed surface can make the surface sticky, vulnerable to fingerprints, and a magnet for dust. Wax-containing products applied over some oils won't adhere properly. Cleaning up the mess may require a lot of elbow grease.

Stains. Consumers Union's tests showed that a supermarket furniture cleaner isn't likely to protect a wood finish against common stains. Moreover, a fresh application of the product is by no means guaranteed to remove any new stains. A bit of ordinary dish-washing liquid and water should do the job just as well. Be sure to pretest to ensure that it does not leave a film behind, which could interfere with bonding of wax and varnish.

Water. Any furniture cleaner should be able to wipe away water spots. But water that's allowed to stand on wood furniture is likely to penetrate most finishes. When you wipe away the water, a cloudy white mark often remains (except solvent-borne urethane cleaners). You may be able to buff out a light mark with a product that has a high oil content. But some rings on certain kinds of furniture finish won't yield—meaning it's time to call in the refinisher.

Scratches. Most furniture-care products don't contain dye, so they aren't meant to cover up deep scratches. Products that claim to hide surface scratches are worth a try. Tests showed that one product, *Oz Cream Polish*, managed to fill in scratches and make them less visible. Sometimes a little acetone can be used to dissolve the lacquer, allowing it to refill the scratches. Here again, pretesting is essential.

RECOMMENDATIONS

For relatively new furniture that's been maintained in good condition, there's no practical reason to add another cleaning product to the clutter under the kitchen sink. It's easy enough to use a little plain water and hand dishwashing liquid to take care of dirtier surfaces. Again, it's a good idea to try any furniture-treatment product on an inconspicuous area before plunging into the job full tilt.

If you want to protect furniture finishes against heat and solvents—such as alcoholic beverages, aftershave lotion, perfume, cough syrup, and the like—the best protection is a nonabsorbent barrier, such as a dish or a coaster.

CARING FOR VALUED FURNITURE OR TEAK FURNITURE

Older furniture that still bears its original finish and teak furniture both require special care. Regular dusting is important for antiques, say the experts. Tools of the trade include feather dusters, soft cotton cloths laundered without harsh detergents, and small vacuum cleaners.

The experts also recommend waxing, but generally only once or twice a year. Some antique dealers recommend waxing at the beginning and end of the heating season. Changes in temperature and humidity can be very damaging to wood furniture because wood shrinks and expands in response to those changes. Waxing unfinished surfaces allows the raw wood to absorb the wax, thereby minimizing the chance that the wood will crack or the veneer will lift or separate. You should wax the underside of a table, for example, as well as the unfinished interior of highboys, breakfronts, and other so-called case pieces.

Some experts recommend against waxes that contain silicone. They say such products compromise the wood's ability to respond to changes in temperature and humidity, and increase the risk of cracking.

Teak, which is an oil-finished product, also has special needs. Some industry experts say frequent dusting is important. Furniture that's used fairly often may need oiling every month or two. The experts recommend a solution of mild detergent for cleaning and tung oil (or equivalent) for restoring the sheen in dry areas.

Teak furniture not subject to much wear may need oiling only a few times a year. If the wood looks pale and the surface feels dry, the furniture probably needs oiling. One teak furniture retailer suggests using a clean, soft cloth to oil the entire piece, then letting the oil sit for three to four hours or, better, overnight. Afterward, buff with another clean, soft cloth to remove excess oil.

UPHOLSTERED FURNITURE

Regular vacuuming is about the best way to keep upholstery looking fresh. But you may not be motivated to vacuum upholstered furniture often enough; dust isn't as obvious on an armchair as it is on a tabletop. Unless upholstered furniture is vacuumed regularly, the material can become so dirty that drastic measures may become necessary.

A surprisingly large number of people take the most drastic measure of all—they just throw out the soiled furniture and replace it with new furniture. According to a survey, that's how a significant number of *Consumer Reports* subscribers dealt with the problem of soil buildup. Some took a less-drastic approach, opting for reupholstering or slipcovers. Still others chose heavy-duty, overall cleaning—a far more economical solution, if it works.

There are three ways to clean upholstered furniture: You

DEALING WITH SPILLS AND STAINS ON LEATHER

Leather dyers either apply a pigmented coating to the leather's surface or treat the hide with aniline dye. Pigmented leather is more resistant to water-soluble spills and stains. Aniline-dyed leather is exceptionally soft and exceptionally porous. Spills soak up quickly, becoming stains that can be almost impossible to remove.

You can test your leather furniture to find out which type of dye was used. Place a drop of water on a location that's not often seen (under the cushion, for example). If the water doesn't soak in, the leather is pigmented. If it does soak in, the leather is aniline dyed—and vulnerable.

Suede is another vulnerable leather—not just because of the dyeing process, but because it's porous and quick to sop up stains. In addition, suede has a nap that's flattened by liquid spills and by use. Only a professional leather refinisher can restore the nap to suede.

Vacuuming is an important part of routine maintenance of leather furniture, whether it's pigmented, aniline dyed, or suede. You can also wipe pigmented leather periodically with a soft white cloth dampened with water. And you can brush suede with a terry-cloth towel to spiff up its nap. Beyond vacuuming, there isn't much you can do for aniline-dyed leather. When it becomes stained or soiled, your only recourse is professional cleaning.

can buy a cleaning product and apply it to the fabric by hand. You can buy or rent a machine that cleans carpets and upholstery. You can call in a professional cleaning service, usually listed under "Carpet Cleaners" or "Upholstery Cleaners" in the Yellow Pages.

Generally, cleaning by hand means spraying upholstery cleaner on the fabric; gently rubbing the resulting foam with a damp

If you spill something on pigmented leather, the faster you clean it up, the better. Consumers Union applied test stains to swatches of pigmented leather and blotted them up a minute later with a damp washcloth. The water-based stains (ketchup, cola, coffee, grape juice, milk, mustard, and red wine) disappeared, but oil-based stains like crayon, ballpoint-pen ink, lipstick, Italian salad dressing, and cream shoe polish did not come off.

Then some commercial leather cleaners were tried to see how they might handle these stubborn stains on pigmented leather. All of the cleaners removed some color.

Don't consider using cleaning solvents, ink removers, or paint removers on pigmented leather. Since the color is essentially painted on the leather, those products can remove color.

When you are faced with stains that won't come out, find a professional. Call the store where you purchased the furniture. If you don't get results, check the Yellow Pages or ask a local dry cleaner for advice. Cleaners who handle leather clothing don't always work on leather furniture, so it may take a few calls to find a leather-furniture cleaner. Expect the cleaning to be costly, and expect to be without your furniture for a while: often, professionals prefer to clean leather in the shop. Removing dirt and stains can also remove dyes, so the furniture may need to be recolored.

sponge, cloth, or brush; and vacuuming the residue. The job can be time-consuming, and the furniture may not turn out clean enough. Any hand cleaning product is likely to work better if the job is done before the upholstery is truly filthy.

Even subscribers who cleaned with a machine weren't always happy with the result, and some found a machine difficult to use. Setting up the machine, cleaning the piece of furniture, and then disassembling and cleaning the machine can be quite a lot of work.

Many subscribers left the cleaning to a professional, but a substantial number indicated that even the pros couldn't get their furniture clean.

PROFESSIONAL CLEANING

Cleaning a six-foot sofa can cost anywhere from $40 to $100, depending on where you live and whom you hire. Replacing a damaged sofa with a new one can cost a lot more, so price shouldn't be the most important criterion when you're hiring a professional; competence should be.

One way to find an upholstery cleaning service, of course, is to look in the phone book, where you'll find listings for big national companies, large regional companies, and local companies. If you come up empty, the International Institute of Carpet and Upholstery Certification can recommend firms that have passed a test on cleaning upholstery. When you call the institute's number (206-693-5675), a representative will use your zip code to locate two or three cleaning firms in your area. Another phone number to remember is the Association of Specialists in Cleaning and Restoration (1-800-272-7012). Both organizations may be able to help with questions regarding stain removal.

Expect any upholstery cleaning firm to give you a preliminary estimate over the phone, then come to the house to evaluate the furniture and spot-test it—by applying a bit of cleaner to an inconspicuous piece of the fabric—before giving a firm price quote.

A reputable company should explain the procedure and tell you what the furniture will look like after cleaning. They should outline their guarantee and voluntarily offer references.

Some professionals may prefer to "steam" clean upholstery with hot water and detergent because the results are generally better than dry cleaning with a solvent. But cleaning with water, even when it's done by a pro, can be a risky business. Therefore, a careful cleaner will spot-test when they come to your home to determine the potential for damage before quoting a firm price. If problems appear as a result of a spot test, a professional cleaner may switch from steam cleaning to dry cleaning.

Some professional cleaners spot-test on the scheduled cleaning day. That's also an acceptable approach, as long as the tested material has time to dry thoroughly—so any defects are visible—before work begins.

Professional carpet and upholstery cleaners may raise the subject of chemical fabric protectors. There is, of course, an extra charge for such treatment, and therefore there are extra profits for the seller. If a protector was applied at the mill where the fabric is made, the fabric shouldn't need to be retreated until it has been cleaned two or three times.

Although there are many brands of stain repellent, there are basically two types: fluorocarbons and silicones. Fluorocarbons (e.g., *Scotchgard* or *Teflon*) protect against both oil- and water-based stains; silicones protect only against water-based stains. Some silicone products may yellow with exposure to ultraviolet light.

If you don't know whether your upholstery has been treated with a stain protector, you might consider having one applied after cleaning. Two caveats: It's important that the protector be applied evenly. (Electric sprayers and aerosol cans are likely to create a more even coat than is possible with a pump sprayer.) And it's important to check the label for precautions. Some protectors are recommended for use only on certain types of fabrics. As with any treatment, it is advisable to apply a bit of protector on a hidden area of the upholstery to make sure the dye doesn't bleed.

RECOMMENDATIONS

Preventive maintenance—vacuuming regularly and catching spills before they become stains—can go a long way toward postponing the need for an overall cleaning. Vacuum all surfaces of the furniture, including the back and sides, the skirt, the arms, the platform underneath the cushions, and both sides of loose cushions.

If you're working on arms that are narrower than the vacuum cleaner's nozzle, cover the exposed section of the nozzle with your hand or a piece of cardboard to improve suction. When vacuuming a delicate fabric—velvet, nubby silk, or crewel embroidery, for instance—you can avoid snagging the fabric by placing a piece of nonmetallic window screen or nylon mesh between the nozzle and the fabric.

Once furniture is too soiled for vacuuming, your best bet is to hire a professional. Choose one who will evaluate the furniture and spot-test the fabric before cleaning. Make sure the company indicates, in writing, any problems anticipated during the cleaning.

You'll save money by doing the job yourself, but your success will depend on your own cleaning skills, and the work takes a lot of time. Spot-test any cleaning product you plan to use before you submit your furniture to a cleaning, and apply the cleaning product in a well-lighted area so you can see how the job is going.

A steamer can be used only on fabrics that can tolerate a water-based cleaner. Additionally, the machine isn't easy to set up, use, and clean. Be careful not to overwet the upholstery, and be very careful with piping. Moisture can cause many types of stuffing to bleed. After using a steamer, open windows and doors and use fans to speed drying. Upholstery should dry in less than 24 hours.

A GUIDE TO UPHOLSTERY FABRICS

Wool, cotton, linen, silk, rayon, nylon, and polyester are among the fibers that are turned into coverings for sofas and chairs. The fabric may be made of a single fiber or a blend, and it may have a special finish, such as the starchy glaze that gives linen its soft glow.

Steam cleaning with detergent and water is an effective way to clean many fabrics. But not all fabrics relate well to water. Some shrink; some become mottled by water spots; some turn brown.

To clean fabric successfully, you must first find out just what kind of fabric you're dealing with. If the furniture was purchased within the last few years, it probably has a cleaning code on its label. (Look under the cushions for a tag affixed to the platform.) A "W" means that the fabric can be cleaned with a water-based product. An "S" indicates that a solvent-based cleaner (dry cleaning) is required. If the code reads "W-S," the choice is yours. An "X" is bad news: Only cleaning by vacuuming is recommended.

The guide to upholstery fabrics on page 40 provides information about the cleaning of materials commonly used in upholstery textiles and can help you decide whether to dry-clean with solvents or "wet clean" with a water-based solution. If your fabric is a blend of different fibers, base your decision on the most sensitive one in the blend.

UPHOLSTERY STAINS

For some furniture, the problem isn't widespread soil but a sudden spill. If you're quick enough, blotting the spill with a clean

A GUIDE TO UPHOLSTERY FABRICS

This guide was published in a February 1992 report.

Fiber. **Cotton** refers to all cotton except Haitian, which may release a brown dye and stretch when wet. All the fibers are likely to be stained by oil-based spills. **Cotton, linen, rayon, silk, wool,** and **nylon** are also likely to be stained by water-based spills. Dry cleaning is acceptable for all the fibers. Wet cleaning, which often works better, is generally OK for all, but check under "wet-cleaning

Fiber		Wet cleaning flaws			
	Bleed	Water-spot	Brown	Shrink	
Cotton	2	Low	High	Moderate	
Linen	2	Low	High	High	
Rayon	2	High	High	Very high	
Silk	1-3	High	High	Low	
Wool	2-3	Low	Moderate	Moderate	
Acetate	4-5	Low	Low	Low	
Acrylic	5	Low	Moderate	Low	
Nylon	4-5	Low	Moderate	Low	
Olefin	5	Low	Low	Low	
Polyester	5	Low	Low	Low	

flaws" to see what problems can arise, and be sure to spot-test.

Tendency to bleed. On a scale from 1 to 5, with 1 most likely to bleed; 5 least likely. Bleeding can occur with either wet or dry cleaning.

Wet-cleaning flaws. The tendency for fibers to water-spot, brown, or shrink during cleaning with a water-based solution. These columns can help you determine whether dry or wet cleaning is more appropriate for your upholstery.

	Comments
	May contain glazing, sizing, or other finishes that can run or be removed during cleaning.
	May contain glazing, sizing, or other finishes that can run or be removed during cleaning.Turns dark when wet; hard to assess quality of cleaning.
	May contain glazing, sizing, or other finishes that can run or be removed during cleaning. Tends to shrink even when preshrunk.
	Water marks may be difficult to remove without damaging fabric. May stretch with excessive agitation.
	Turns dark when wet; hard to assess quality of cleaning.
	Tends to shrink even when preshrunk. Dissolves in acetone. Avoid nail-polish remover and commercial ink removers.
	Spots may reappear after cleaning.
	Dissolves in strong acids.
	Spots may reappear after cleaning. Latex backing may be weakened by age, sunlight, and chlorinated solvents. Resists bleach.
	Spots may reappear after cleaning.

white towel or white (no pattern) paper towels may do the trick. (A white towel lets you see what you're removing and eliminates the chance of introducing another stain in the form of a dye.) Once a spill becomes a stain, cleanup can still be successful, if you use the right approach. Certain basics apply to all stain-removal efforts. For recommended cleaning agents and techniques for removing a variety of stains from both washable and unwashable fabrics, refer to Appendix B: Stain Removal.

House Cleaning

ALL-PURPOSE CLEANERS

A good all-purpose liquid cleaner should be able to handle a variety of chores but may not be really useful for all purposes. Most, for example, lack the special qualities required to clean windows and ovens or remove mildew. But all-purpose cleaners are versatile enough for mopping, washing, and spot-cleaning hard surfaces such as walls, floors, appliances, kitchen cabinets, and countertops. All-purpose cleaners are often the type of product needed when water won't do.

SPOT CLEANING

Of the two types of all-purpose cleaners available, the "pourables" (liquids applied on grime) generally have stronger formulations and do better overall spot cleaning than spray cleaners—which at best turn in just an adequate job. Top-performing pourables often contain pine oil, an effective cleaning ingredient with a distinctive scent of pine associated with the impression of cleanliness.

FLOOR MOPPING

Pourable products when diluted in a bucket of water can also be effective for mopping floors. Few spray products suggest that their liquid contents can be used in a similar manner. For floor mopping, effective pourables often claim to contain pine oil, citrus oil, or oil soap.

DAMAGE TO SURFACES

When used at full strength, an all-purpose cleaner should be used gently, then promptly and carefully rinsed off. Otherwise, you may risk marring the surface being cleaned. Check the label for precautions; if in doubt, first test the cleaner on an inconspicuous place for marring.

SAFETY TO USERS

Some products are caustic enough to warrant your using rubber gloves when cleaning, or at least avoiding prolonged contact with the skin. Since the solvents and other ingredients that dissolve, emulsify, suspend, or otherwise loosen grime are powerful chemicals, any cleaner should be used carefully in accordance with its labeled precautions and kept out of the reach of children. To avoid potentially hazardous chemical reactions, never mix any cleaner with anything other than water.

RECOMMENDATIONS

It's handy to have both types of all-purpose cleaners: a spray for quick point-and-shoot cleaning and a pourable for mopping and heavy-duty spot cleaning. Spot cleaning can always be improved, within limits, with the application of elbow grease, prompt rinsing, and plenty of clean wipes.

Most pourable cleaners may be diluted for cleaning walls and floors with a sponge or a mop and bucket, and many should do a respectable job. Some pourables and sprays are labeled as disinfectants. At best, however, such cleaners can only temporarily reduce populations of some germs in a limited area for a limited time.

BATHROOM CLEANERS

Some of the products promoted as bathroom cleaners derive most of their strength from old-fashioned pine oil; others rely on a mix of other powerful chemicals. Because damp bathrooms are fertile ground for fungi, bathroom cleaners often claim to contain an anti-mildew agent, an ingredient some all-purpose cleaners lack.

Per use, some bathroom cleaners cost up to twice as much as some all-purpose cleaners. Manufacturers try to justify the higher cost with fancy packaging. Trigger spray pumps, aerosol cans, and flip-top containers are more convenient than the screw-top containers that hold some all-purpose cleaners; there's no pouring involved, so spills are less likely.

EFFECTIVENESS ON SOAP SCUM

Most bathroom cleaners and all general-purpose cleaners are highly effective at cleaning soap scum. For really difficult-to-clean surfaces, you can improve the product's performance by leaving it on the soap scum slightly longer than the time recommended on the label.

EFFECTIVENESS ON MILDEW

Despite label claims, few bathroom cleaners are very effective at removing mildew. Most products including all-purpose cleaners are largely ineffective in getting rid of mildew that accumulates in the grout on a tiled surface. A better approach is to apply an effective cleaner before mildew has accumulated. Common household chlorine bleach is highly effective and economical for killing and removing mildew (refer to the section on Bleaches).

Many cleaners claim to disinfect, and they may indeed get rid of some microorganisms for a while. But trying to kill microorganisms in an unsterile environment is futile. As soon as you eliminate some germs, they're replaced by others.

Surface Damage

You may spill a bit of cleaner and not notice the spill for hours. Quite a few products dull or discolor brass and painted trim. Some also mar stainless steel surfaces and, rarely, you may find one that also mars vinyl shower curtains.

Some cleaning products can irritate skin and eyes. A few are alkaline or acidic enough to warrant the use of rubber gloves.

Some pump spray products can irritate lungs. A few specifically warn against use by anyone with heart or respiratory problems.

Generally, bathroom cleaners are not too hazardous for a healthy, reasonably cautious person to use, but read labels carefully.

A cleaner containing bleach shouldn't be mixed with a product containing ammonia or acid. Such combinations can produce irritating fumes.

Recommendations

Specialized bathroom cleaners are convenient to use, and some are very effective on soap scum and mildew. But a good all-purpose cleaner can cost less, clean soap scum at least as well, and may also do a good job of inhibiting the growth of mildew.

Disposable wet towelettes are unnecessary, even if they are handy for small jobs. Most are fairly expensive, considering that you're likely to use them only for light cleaning on small areas.

Drain Cleaners

Most people give very little thought to their household pipes until one or more of their drains stops working. Then, they face a choice of several unappealing remedies: Call the plumber, wrestle with a plunger or a plumber's "snake," or don protective gear and pour in some chemical drain cleaner. A fourth remedy, one of the new biological treatments on the market, may help keep drains clear, but it's not good at breaking up an existing clog.

This book doesn't offer any panaceas, just advice on the best options available for do-it-yourself drain care. As a plumber might tell you, the typical kitchen clog differs from a bathroom blockage. Kitchen drains are chiefly plagued by vegetable scraps and congealed fats. Bathroom drains tend to clog with soap scum and hair.

The first order of business on a drain should be preventive maintenance (see section on "Maintaining the Free-Flowing Drain"). There, biological treatments, designed to speed up the slow but still flowing drain, can be useful. But if a drain clogs completely, turn to a plunger, snake, or other mechanical device. If that approach fails, and it's a sink drain that's clogged, you might consider removing the U-shaped trap in the pipes where sink clogs often lodge (or removing the cleanout plug, if the trap has one). Consider a chemical cleaner only if all else has failed. Its powerful ingredients can cause serious harm if inhaled or accidentally brought into contact with the skin or eyes. And if the chemical cleaner doesn't budge the clog, you'll be left with a corrosive mess to clean up.

MAINTAINING THE FREE-FLOWING DRAIN

A few preventive measures will limit the likelihood that you'll have a clogged drain.

- Avoid pouring grease down the kitchen sink.
- Be sure sinks, tubs, and showers have strainers to trap food, hair, and the like. Regularly clean the strainers, and periodically remove and clean the drain-plug mechanism in bathroom sinks and tubs. That mechanism is a common place for hair that can escape the strainer to lodge and form an obstruction. The hair,

in turn, can become a filter for soap, skin oils, and other residues carried by the water.

■ Pouring hot water into a drain is unlikely to clear a clog, but a weekly dose of boiling water can be effective to maintain a freely running drain. Heat about a gallon of water, pour in half, wait a few minutes, and then pour in the rest. Be careful to pour the water directly down the drain, not on the basin, tub, or toilet. Boiling water could crack the porcelain; it can also inactivate a biological drain opener. So do not use hot water any sooner than the residence time mandated by the biological drain opener's directions.

BIOLOGICAL TREATMENTS

Household drains rarely clog without warning. Unless suddenly blocked by an object, they tend to run slower as impediments accumulate. Biological drain treatments are designed to keep pipes cleaner and clearer by introducing bacteria that feed on the organic matter in those accumulations.

Biological treatments are often marketed as a safer alternative to pouring chemical cleaners down your drains (a reasonable claim, given the chemicals' proven hazards). Some treatments are sold through catalogs that specialize in "environmentally friendly" products; others are sold in hardware and grocery stores.

Some treatments claim to use enzymes to stage an initial hit-and-run attack on organic matter in the pipes, notably grease and soap. But the real muscle in biological treatments comes from microorganisms that break down and digest that organic material. The bugs eventually flourish in the pipes to provide a continuous, live-in cleanup crew.

Microorganisms don't eat just anything. Hair, for example, being rather indigestible, is not on their menu. But the bacteria in the treatments do eat away at the sticky organic stuff that often binds hair and other materials together, or the material that holds it to pipes. It takes time for the bugs to reach their full effectiveness. All the biologicals Consumers Union tested require at least one overnight application, during which time the drain cannot be used. Most treatments require two to five initial applications to get the bug colony established. After that, some bacteria are regularly washed out as the drain is used, so all treatments recommend a regular monthly "maintenance" application. Avoid pouring boiling water, bleach, disinfectants, solvents, and other enemies of bacteria into a treated drain.

Don't expect results from a biological treatment when a drain is blocked by an obstruction made of wood, plastic, or some other material not in the bugs' diet.

While they are noncorrosive, biological treatments are not entirely benign. The packaging for most biologicals warns of harm from swallowing, and some labels also recommend avoiding contact with skin, eyes, and respiratory passages.

MECHANICAL OPENERS

Drain clogs are subject to two kinds of physical assault by the mechanical devices tested by Consumers Union: pressure from a pump, hose-end bladder, or plunger, and drilling through by a plumber's auger, also known as a "snake."

All the mechanical openers should work fine on a soft, fatty kitchen clog. But the pumps and plungers may not be able to cope reliably with a bathroom clog (which may be a concoction of such materials as facial tissue, toilet tissue, soap, toothpaste, and human hair). Snakes, however, should have no such trouble. They snag onto the meshed hair and haul out the entire plug.

All the mechanical devices are safe enough to use, but all do require some strength and skill to use effectively. And each type has its drawbacks. The auger must be threaded through openings in any cross bars or strainers, and the holes may be too small to accommodate the cable tip. Also, the auger must be turned as it's fed into the pipe, a task that's sometimes hard for one person to accomplish. No auger can be used through a garbage-disposal unit, and some may even have trouble negotiating the trap below the sink. (They can, however, be fed into the open pipe after the trap is removed.)

Hose-end bladders can't be used at all through crossbars or strainers. And a plunger (or any other pressure device) is ineffective if the drain has a vent between the sink and the clog that can't be sealed when the device is used. (Duct tape or a wet rag makes an effective temporary seal for the vents usually found below the faucet in bathroom sinks and tubs.)

It makes sense to keep a couple of mechanical drain openers around the house. A snake is the most versatile device, since it can both break up a greasy clog and snag clumps of hair. Unlike a pressure device such as a plunger, the snake can remove all or part of a blockage, limiting the chance that the clog will be liberated only to flow down the drain and cause trouble elsewhere.

Among the pressure devices, a plunger is the best bet for reasons of price, convenience, and versatility. Any plunger can be used on a sink or tub blockage. However, those models with a fold-out cup have the edge when tackling toilet clogs.

CHEMICAL CLEANERS

Chemical drain cleaners are among the most hazardous products sold for household use. All highly corrosive, they can injure eyes and mucous membranes on contact, and ordinary skin in only seconds. Chemical drain cleaners include liquid lye-and-bleach mixes and granular lyes, which are strongly alkaline, and concentrated liquid acids.

Even when diluted, chemical drain cleaners can attack not only the organic matter in clogs but also metal pipes (especially the thin brass pipes often found under sinks) and porcelain surfaces. The heat the cleaners release as they work may soften plastic pipes and weaken the cemented joints between them. In fact, concentrated sulfuric acid can release so much heat in a drain that the liquid boils, which may send a small geyser of corrosive liquid back out of the drain.

Worst of all, a chemical drain opener may not work and will leave you with a blocked drain full of corrosive liquid. That's especially likely if the blockage lies not in the U-shaped trap under the fixture but farther along in the pipe, where the cleaner may never reach.

Even if the chemicals do make it to the clog, they're likely to do a mediocre job at best. That ho-hum performance makes it all too likely that several applications of a cleaner will be required to clear a clog, further compounding the hazards of using one of these products.

The granular lye products may even create their own blockages. If you pour in more than the recommended amount, there's a chance the granules will form a solid mass. You or the plumber may then be forced to remove the original obstruction and the cake of lye.

Safer drain cleaners that use noncorrosive solvents in place of lye and acid have reached the market in recent years. But none has succeeded in Consumers Union's tests.

Consumers Union is reluctant to recommend any chemical drain cleaner, either for tackling a clog or (as some manufacturers recommend) as preventive medicine for slow drains, and strongly advises against acid-based drain cleaners. Concentrated sulfuric or hydrochloric acid is too risky for amateurs to use and too dangerous to keep around the house, especially if there are children about.

SAFETY

The labels of chemical drain cleaners contain multiple warnings and precautions. In the case of accidental personal contact with a chemical drain cleaner, immediately flush the area with copious amounts of cool water and continue to do so while someone contacts a poison control center or a medical doctor for instructions.

GARBAGE BAGS

Plastic garbage bags didn't even exist 30 years ago. People typically reused paper grocery bags for their kitchen scraps and burned yard waste, raked it into the street, or threw it into large metal trash cans. Then they got on with their lives.

You can still reuse other types of bags, of course, but most Americans don't: Nearly 8 in 10 consider plastic garbage bags a household staple. If you're among them, you've probably found that choosing a bag may mean deciding among hundreds of brands.

Why the proliferation? Manufacturers are trying to grab shelf space from competitors and ring up higher sales by adding anything shoppers might favor, whether it's a drawstring closure, a scent designed to ward off animals, or a pastel color.

The confusion doesn't end there. Garbage bags are marketed under different names: trash, rubbish, scrap, wastebasket, kitchen, lawn, and leaf; and on variations of those themes: tall kitchen, large kitchen, and large trash and lawn bags. That makes it easy to pick up the wrong size. What's more, bag size may vary con-

HOW "GREEN" IS MY GARBAGE?

Garbage bags themselves are an example of wasteful consumption, since they're designed to be used once and thrown away. The U.S. Environmental Protection Agency estimates that plastic-bag waste takes up 2.4 percent of all landfill space.

One "green" option, of course, is to reuse bags you already have instead of buying new ones. Nearly any bag from a department store or grocery store is suitable for paper or other dry, lightweight waste. Plastic supermarket bags are fine for food scraps. And those bags are free.

Manufacturers can reduce the environmental impact of newly minted bags by using less plastic. Some manufacturers use recycled plastic (from 10 percent to 100 percent). That includes pre-consumer waste (scrap from the manufacture of other products) as well as postconsumer waste (used milk containers, detergent bottles, grocery sacks, and the like). None of the bags have 100 percent postconsumer waste in their recycled plastic.

How does recycled plastic affect strength? Consumers Union compared test data from bags that claimed to have recycled content with data from bags that make no such claim. Although bags with a small amount of recycled material were as strong and puncture-resistant as bags that make no claim, those with 80 percent or more recycled plastic weren't as tough as the others.

Some towns require yard waste to be put in paper bags, not plastic, because the material is earmarked for composting. Consumers Union tested those bags, too. They're essentially puncture proof and are highly resistant to damage when dropped or dragged. That makes them capable of handling bushes, thorns, or any debris that's sharp or jagged. Keep filled paper bags under cover, though: Once they're wet, they're weaker.

siderably within those groups. As a result, matching the bag to the trash container can be tricky.

The latest marketing wrinkle targets the "green" consumer. No, the issue isn't degradability anymore. (The Federal Trade Commission cracked down on unsubstantiated degradability claims a few years back, and garbage-bag manufacturers have changed their pitch.) Now, many of them tout the use of recycled plastic. That's laudable. However, the trend toward more environmentally friendly products is driven by government regulation as much as by anything else.

How do you tell which bag is most robust? You might think that the number of plies, sometimes noted on the package, is a reliable barometer. Not necessarily, according to Consumers Union tests. Nor is there a clear correlation between the thickness of the plastic and the bag's quality. Some bags boast that they're extra-heavy duty, or made of high-performance or concentrated plastic. When scrutinized by Consumers Union engineers, however, many bags, and their claims, didn't pass muster.

To find out which claims are worth listening to and which bags are worth buying, Consumers Union sent shoppers in 14 states to buy bags. The 55 products they found included name brands, store brands, and bags from mail-order catalogs. For comparison

A NUMBERS GAME?

TYPE OF BAG	USUAL CAPACITY
Waste	4–8 gal.
Tall kitchen	13 gal.
Trash	30–33 gal.
Lawn and leaf	39 gal.

purposes, a paper lawn and leaf bag was also tested; in many towns, residents are required to use such bags.

Consumers Union subjected the bags to laboratory tests and asked staffers to use them at home. In most cases, staffers' judgments and lab results agreed.

Most garbage bags will work fine if used to hold only lightweight trash. If you need a bag that can handle heavier stuff, keep several things in mind:

- You can't judge a bag by its price or name. Inexpensive bags sold by mass merchandisers and by supermarkets sometimes outperformed the nationally advertised brands.
- Some bags that did well overall didn't do well in every test.
- The quality of particular brands wasn't always consistent from size to size.
- Some individual products performed inconsistently from bag to bag.

SIZING THEM UP

The table on page 54 shows the typical categories and sizes of garbage bags. Some makers, however, tag their bags with labels that confound the issue.

All the kitchen bags tested mated easily with the standard kitchen wastebasket. Best are those with a star-shaped seam at their base instead of the usual horizontal seam. They sit flush against the bottom of the wastebasket.

Most trash bags claim to fit inside 30-gallon garbage cans. In reality, many fit, but barely, and not without a struggle. Such problems exist because garbage-can capacity is measured in different ways when filled to the brim or with the lid on, for instance. And cans rated at the same capacity come in different heights, widths, and shapes. As long as no industry standard exists, some bags won't fit some cans.

THICK OR THIN?

Common sense suggests that thicker is better, but that's not always true. The type of plastic, the quality and amount of recycled material, and the manufacturing process also come into play. Kitchen bags measuring ½ mil (a mil is a thousandth of an inch) thick were sometimes tougher than bags twice as thick.

To further muddle the picture, Consumers Union often found the same brand in two labeled thicknesses, depending on where the bags were purchased.

Thickness claims may also be misstated. Consumers Union measured 20 samples of each brand with an electronic caliper and discovered that eight brands, mostly lawn and leaf bags, were significantly thinner than the manufacturer had noted.

PLASTICS

Most garbage bags are made from one of three polyethylene resins. Some brands specify their type of plastic; with others, you can often tell by feeling the bag. It can pay to know, because the type of plastic has some bearing on how well a bag will stand up in use.

Bags made of low-density polyethylene (LDPE) are soft and pliable. Those made of linear low-density polyethylene (LLDPE) are stretchier. Their main asset: resistance to tearing. Bags made of high-density polyethylene (HDPE) are stiffer and more translucent than the others, and they crunch like tissue paper when touched. Because the material is inherently tough and resists punctures, HDPE bags can be made thinner than others without compromising strength. One drawback with HDPE: A little nick easily turns into a big rip.

CLOSING TIME

Most bags come with wire twist ties, plastic key-lock tabs, or some variation of a drawstring. Twist ties provide a tight seal and are simple to use: Merely wrap one around the neck of the bag and give it a couple of turns. On the other hand, twist ties are sometimes too short to wrap securely around a bag. And they're easy to lose.

With plastic tabs, you thread one end through a loop at the other end, then pull. Like twist ties, tabs are easily lost. And as you'll find out, if you try to add another crumpled napkin to a sealed bag once locked, they're hard to unlock.

Staffers who used bags at home liked drawstrings because they're easy to manipulate and there are no small parts to lose. Once the bag is full, you tug and knot the string to close it. On the other hand, the seal may not close completely. Trash and odors may escape; moisture and animal scavengers may get inside. Drawstrings also can be flimsy. During drag-and-drop tests, Consumers Union hoisted the bags by their drawstrings. Some stretched like Silly Putty; others snapped apart.

Less common are handle ties, which look like suspenders atop the bag's shoulders. You close a handle tie by knotting the two loops like the laces of a shoe. That ensures a tight seal. Draping the handles around a container can be a problem, though.

DISPENSE WITH IT

Garbage bags usually come folded and packaged in cartons. You remove them from the box as you would tissues, one at a time. More of a chore are bags that are packaged in a roll and connected by perforations. You pull the end of the roll through a slit in the packaging and tear off the next bag. Some staffers who used those bags at home complained that the rolls unfurled or that it was hard to tear off just one bag.

HANDHELD VACUUM CLEANERS

The most popular type of handheld vacuum operates on rechargeable batteries and can be carried easily from room to room. But hand vacuums with cords offer serious competition, since they can extend vacuuming beyond the length of time that a typical rechargeable model allows.

Handheld vacuums offer extras such as revolving power brushes to beat dirt out of carpeting, as well as an assortment of attachments and extensions designed especially for nooks, crannies, drapes, and ceilings. In addition, cordless models come with a wall-mounted storage bracket that has a built-in battery charger. Car vacuums, which plug into an automobile's cigarette-lighter socket, look much like the cordless models, but they come without a wall storage bracket.

CLEANING ABILITY

Most cordless models rely solely on suction to do the job. The suction end typically tapers to an oblong slot some three inches wide.

Plug-in models, on the other hand, generally provide wider coverage. They often come with a built-in five- or six-inch revolving brush well suited to cleaning rugs. The plug-ins tend to be heavier than the cordless models and auto vacuums.

Consumers Union tested cleaning ability with a variety of soils spread across a smooth wood surface that simulated hardwood flooring. A hand vacuum should be able to deal with such items as granulated sugar, rice, and bread crumbs.

Low-pile carpeting littered with tougher material, however, highlighted the advantage most plug-in models enjoy over their cordless cousins. To retrieve, say, potting soil from a carpet, most cordless vacuums and car vacuums need 20 to 30 passes; a good plug-in model, with its spinning brushes, may need just 5 to 10 passes. Hand vacuums without revolving brushes have a tougher time with beach sand.

Gravel may destroy plastic fan blades or scrape particles of plastic from the innards of some plug-in models. Cordless or car

---

WHEN BATTERIES GO BAD

The rechargeable nickel-cadmium batteries in cordless hand vacuums should accept hundreds of charges. But eventually the clock runs out even on those batteries. In the past, Consumers Union testers have found that batteries are difficult to replace in many hand-vacuum models.

Having a manufacturer's service center replace the batteries can vary greatly in price. Spending, say, $15 to replace the batteries in, say, a $70 or $80 appliance makes sense. But hand vacuums often cost much less than that, so in some cases it may pay simply to replace the entire vacuum.

A decision to throw away the vacuum poses an environmental problem. The cadmium in nicad batteries is toxic and can leach out of landfills to contaminate groundwater supplies. Incineration can release the metals into the air, an even greater hazard.

Some companies will accept their old cordless products for proper disposal. Check with the manufacturer before you trash an appliance.

A growing number of states require that the batteries in cordless appliances be easy to remove so they can be disposed of separately. Consumers Union recommends that you consider ease of battery removal and cost of battery replacement when purchasing any rechargeable appliance.

vacuums won't suffer similar damage, since their filter cup intercepts large debris before it reaches any moving parts.

CONVENIENCE

A revolving brush gives the plug-in vacuums an edge in cleaning carpeting, but it's a mixed blessing. The action of the brush is so vigorous in some models that it competes with their suction, flinging coarser soils about instead of helping to ingest them. Here are some other factors to consider:

Edge cleaning. The narrow nozzle of most cordless models can slip into tighter spots than can the broad brush head of the plug-in models.

Fallout. Most vacuums have a trap or a flap in the intake designed to prevent debris from dropping back onto the floor when the vacuum is switched off. None works perfectly.

Blowby. Sometimes the filters in these vacuums don't stop dust or grit from shooting out through vent holes. It's a good idea to wear eye protection when you vacuum coarse debris.

Noise. The noise these vacuums make measured at arm's length with a sound-level meter tends to track their cleaning prowess (the louder they are the better they clean), especially with plug-in models. The noisiest are about as loud as a regular vacuum cleaner.

FEATURES

Some of the vacuums include attachments that can change their basic character. There may be, for instance, a snap-on revolving brush to convert an ordinary vacuum snout of a cordless model into a vacuuming carpet sweeper, like that on most plug-in models. But the add-on piece places a heavy burden on the batteries, significantly reducing their ability to run the cleaner before an overnight charge is needed.

A few plug-in models work the opposite way: An accessory hose lets you convert a built-in revolving brush to a suction-only nozzle.

Here are some other noteworthy features to consider:

Dual speeds. Several vacuums offer two motor settings. Others let you reduce suction by opening an air intake. Less suction may be useful for vacuuming curtains, blinds, or loose-fitting upholstery.

Brushes, wands, nozzles. On a power-brush model, snap-on dust brushes let you gently rake upholstery. And on suction-only models, they improve carpet cleaning by stirring up the embedded litter. A wandlike crevice tool powerfully focuses suction in small areas, while a broad floor nozzle lets you cover more area quicker.

RECOMMENDATIONS

A power cord would seem to compromise the main advantage of a handheld vacuum. But an extra-long cord (some are 25 feet) may make a plug-in vacuum an attractive alternative to a cordless model.

Plug-in models are strong performers, and some provide much greater dirt capacity than that available with a cordless vacuum.

DEALING WITH WET SPILLS

A few cordless vacuums are wet/dry models. They're designed to sip up the proverbial spilled milk, or even the contents of a tipped goldfish bowl. Since they are cordless, there's no shock hazard.

You should clean the vacuum (a messy job) after every wet use, lest the soggy contents turn stagnant. It might be easier to use a sponge in the first place.

Most have a broad revolving brush, which helps them make quick work of a variety of soils ground into a rug.

OVEN CLEANERS

Use oven cleaners only on shiny porcelain-coated metal surfaces, or glass. Never use them on continuous-cleaning (dull finish) or self-cleaning oven finishes or on bare metal.

Some oven-cleaning products contain lye, one of the most dangerous substances sold for household use. Baked-on oven dirt is too tough for ordinary cleaners. Lye causes a chemical reaction, decomposing the stuck-on fats and sugars into soapy compounds you can wash away. Lye-containing oven cleaners are corrosively alkaline and reactive enough to cause serious burns, which is why labels on such products contain long lists of warnings.

Some oven cleaners on the market are aerosol sprays, which are convenient to apply but hard to aim neatly. Clouds of aerosol mist deposit cleaner not only on oven walls but perhaps also on heating elements, thermostats, and light fixtures, and in your lungs. Such product labels warn you not to inhale the fumes. But some other application methods and container designs protect you better.

Still, any product that contains lye must be used with extreme caution. Lye can burn skin and eyes. Inhaled droplets can actually burn the throat and lungs. Before using any cleaner containing lye, you should don safety goggles, a long-sleeved shirt, and rubber gloves. If you're using an aerosol, you should also wear a paper dust mask (to keep from inhaling the droplets) along with protective goggles.

Not only should you take steps to protect yourself from the corrosive effects of lye, you should protect nearby floors, counters, and other surfaces. Spread newspaper on the floor in front of the oven. Take care not to splash any of the cleaner on aluminum, copper, or painted surfaces outside the oven, and keep it off the heating element, gaskets, and light fixture inside the oven.

Another way to avoid dangerous fumes and corrosive spatters is to use an aerosol cleaner without lye. Instead of using lye to break down oven grime, such products use a combination of organic surfactants that are activated by heat. This type of product doesn't have to carry a long list of warnings on its label. It isn't likely to damage kitchen surfaces. You don't have to arm yourself with rubber gloves and a face mask to use it because it isn't likely to irritate.

PACKAGING

An oven cleaner's packaging affects its convenience of use and safety. Oven-cleaning products come in several forms such as pad, aerosol, brush-on jelly, and pump spray. All have drawbacks.

Because they don't create airborne lye particles, pads are a relatively safe way to apply oven cleaner, as long as you've covered your hands and forearms. Aerosols are easy to apply, but they're also easy to get on gaskets, heating elements, and sometimes your face by mistake. A broad, concave button makes it harder to misdirect the spray than a small button.

Not only is it tedious to paint an entire oven with brush-on jelly, it's almost impossible to keep the jelly from spattering. Finally, a hand-pumped spray can be a real annoyance. Some products have an adjustable nozzle that produces anything from a stream to a misty, broad spray. The stream doesn't cover much and it splatters, and the spray is unnecessarily diffuse and easy to inhale.

RECOMMENDATIONS

The instructions that come with self-cleaning ovens warn against using commercial oven cleaners. Wording varies, but a basic warning reads "Do not use commercial oven cleaners or oven protective coatings around any part of the self-cleaning oven." This is because the cleaners may damage the porcelain finish during the high-temperature cleaning cycle.

Even if you lack a self-cleaning or continuous-cleaning oven, you aren't necessarily sentenced to the hard labor of cleaning your oven. An oven in continual use can reach a steady state at which grease and grime burn off at the same rate they accumulate. Serious spills, such as when a cake overflows its pan, can be scraped up after the oven cools. A little dirt in the oven never hurt anybody; a little oven cleaner might. So you can skip using an oven cleaner. But if you feel otherwise, then choose a noncaustic oven cleaner.

PAPER TOWELS

Some brands of paper towel are available nationwide, but there are many regional and store brands, too. In some cases, towels of a nationally known brand may vary somewhat from region to region.

Manufacturers try to control a larger share of the market by selling a variety of brands, aiming a premium one, for example, at consumers who believe that a high price connotes high quality and aiming a moderately priced one at consumers who treat one roll of towels pretty much like any other. One supermarket executive termed premium-priced towels "overspecified"—meaning they are thicker and heavier than they need to be. The overspecified towel gives the advertiser something to brag about and helps justify the generally higher price, which in turn pays for both the manufacturing costs and the heavy advertising and promotion expenses.

Paper towels lead a brief and unglamorous life. They're typically called upon to scour a dirty oven, sop up a kitchen spill, or wipe a window, and then within moments they're gone. And yet, to perform these seemingly unexacting tasks, paper towels need disparate qualities:

- Even when wet, they should withstand scrubbing without falling apart.
- For mopping up, a costly but highly absorbent towel can be as economical as a cheap but less absorbent towel. For spilled salad dressing or motor oil, a poor-quality towel may smear the spill rather than absorb it.

But for many other uses, most products will do the job.

Towels should separate cleanly at their perforations; otherwise, you may be left holding either a torn sheet or more sheets than you need. Generally, the two-ply towels detach more evenly than the one-ply towels.

Paper towels with short, weakly anchored fibers tend to shed lint, a particular problem when you clean a mirror or windowpane.

Softness is relatively unimportant in a paper towel, at least according an informal poll of more than 60 Consumers Union staffers. Soft towels are usually more absorbent, but they may not hold up as well during scouring.

RECOMMENDATIONS

The strongest, most absorbent towels are likely to be the premium-priced brands. Use an economical one for everyday chores. For more demanding tasks—like picking up a large spill or cleaning a carpet—you might want to buy a roll of strong and absorbent, relatively expensive towels to keep around the house.

Paper towels are the second largest "loss leader" in stores. Wait for a sale of your favorite product and stock up with enough to last you until the next sale.

USING PAPER TOWELS WITH MICROWAVE OVENS

For modest microwaving chores like steaming fish or poultry, cooking vegetables or bacon, or preparing hot sandwiches, it's wise to wrap or cover the food with white paper towels. They keep the oven clean by absorbing spattered grease and excess moisture and help to keep certain foods from drying out or becoming soggy. But are some paper towels better than others for microwaving?

Some manufacturers sell brands that they claim are specially formulated for microwave tasks. "Microwave" paper-towel brands are identical to their regular siblings except that they are claimed to be food grade (FDA approved for food contact), having fewer heavy metals. But for simple microwaving, there is no need to pay extra for these specialty products. Any strong, absorbent, plain white (unprinted) paper towel should do.

TOUGHER TOWELS FOR TOUGH JOBS

Shop towels are for cleaning up grime in the garage or workshop, scrubbing away rust, and other tasks too tough for ordinary paper towels. Shop towels made of paper are throwaways; cloth towels are meant to be washed and reused.

Shop towels tend to be stronger than most ordinary paper towels. Of course, cloth shop towels are far stronger than any of the paper products.

Both paper and cloth shop towels clean greasy tools and effectively scrub rust. Some ordinary paper towels might tend to shred a bit but should do the job nevertheless.

Paper shop towels absorb water faster than their cloth counterparts. After several washings to remove their sizing, the cloth shop towels still don't absorb water as quickly but are fine for oil.

Paper shop towels are certainly more convenient than cloth. But the cloth shop towels are cheaper if they're used at least 10 times. (Household rags, of course, are cheaper still.)

SCOURING CLEANSERS

It used to be that the more abrasive a scouring powder was, the more effectively it cleaned and the more surely it eroded porcelain-enamel finishes and the decorative polish of cookware and acrylic vanities.

Today's cleansers claim to remove soil and stains without damaging the surface being cleaned. Liquid cleansers, introduced in the 1970s, replaced gritty particles, such as silica, with softer abrasives like calcium carbonate. Today, both liquids and powders derive much of their cleaning strength from detergent, bleach, and other alkaline or acidic ingredients. The detergent in the cleanser helps loosen soil and cut grease; the bleach aids in removing many stains, especially from scratched and dented surfaces; and the other ingredients enhance a cleanser's effectiveness on a variety of stains.

The gentlest cleansers will leave few or no marks even on a piece of glass (similar in hardness to the porcelain in bathtubs and sinks). A slightly abrasive cleanser leaves light hairline scratches on glass panels and is more likely to erode surfaces over time. Moderately abrasive cleansers leave a silky smooth frosting of scratches, although nothing like the deep marks left by old-time abrasive cleansers.

A good product, if inadvertently spilled and not wiped up,

shouldn't leave marks on chrome, imitation marble (usually acrylic), fiberglass, glass, or glazed tile. But watch your pots and pans: A number of cleansers dull or discolor aluminum, copper, or other metals if not wiped off after application.

Most cleansers do well on difficult-to-remove soil and on a variety of stains such as pot marks and tea stains on a kitchen sink. Some are especially effective on particular types of difficult stains (such as rust and hard-water deposits) and are labeled accordingly.

SAFETY

Cleansers containing bleach or acid shouldn't be mixed with ammonia or other cleansers—the combination can produce dangerous fumes. Cleansers usually warn about this on the label.

Some cleansers are strongly alkaline or acidic and could irritate your skin. You might also want to remove your jewelry and wear rubber gloves when cleaning with them.

Be especially careful in the use and storage of rust-removing cleansers. They may contain oxalic acid. If so, they will provide warnings regarding the hazards involved.

When you're cleaning a new surface or using a new cleanser, first try it on an inconspicuous corner, wipe it off, and check for marring. Over time, of course, even a gentle product may cause some damage, which is why it's important to use a light touch and a soft applicator, and wipe residues up after each use.

For cleaning with a light touch, apply the cleanser with a cellulose sponge. If this fails on a very soiled surface, cautiously try a more aggressive applicator (e.g., steel wool or copper mesh pads), a plastic mesh pad, or a reinforced sponge.

RECOMMENDATIONS

Today's cleansers tend to be very good to excellent in overall cleaning ability. They range in abrasiveness from negligible to slight to moderate. Liquid cleansers tend to have the lowest abrasiveness, while powders occur at all levels. For delicate surfaces, first try the cleanser in an inconspicuous place.

A barely abrasive product can do an excellent cleaning job, even on tough soils. If you have some very demanding jobs, like scraping crusted soil off old pots and pans or cleaning a badly abraded porcelain sink, you will probably need a moderately abrasive product. If you have rust or hard-water stains, you might consider special cleansers labeled for this purpose.

Cleansers are not appropriate for all chores in the kitchen and bathroom. You'll want a good all-purpose cleaner to take care of ordinary soil on floors, walls, countertops, range surfaces, and the like.

TOILET BOWL CLEANERS

A common cause of persistent toilet-bowl staining is minerals that build up around the waterline and under the rim. The culprit is usually hard water, which has a high mineral content. As the water evaporates, minerals such as whitish calcium or magnesium compounds and rust-colored iron compounds are left behind, coating the upper part of the bowl and eventually hardening into a scale. Even with soft water, molds can form a dark coating in the bowl. If the ceramic surface is slick, such deposits hardly find a foothold. But if the surface has been scratched by abrasive cleaners or roughened with age, the buildup can grow rapidly.

Automatic, in-tank cleaners are the easiest to use but generally only mask the dirt. The "real" cleaners are the liquid and granular in-bowl cleaners that are meant to be used with a brush.

IN-BOWL CLEANERS

Most in-bowl cleaners use acid to dissolve mineral scale and eradicate stains. Active agents may include hydrochloric, phosphoric, or oxalic acids; some granular cleaners use sodium bisulfate, which when dissolved works like acid. Brands with the highest acidity have the greatest potential for cleaning. Products with lower acid content may require more cleaner, more time, or more muscle to do the job.

Nonacidic liquids may not be very effective at removing mineral stains. But they should work well on nonmineral stains that can be brushed away readily.

You might try a dash of liquid all-purpose cleaner. Brushed on, it can clean a lightly soiled bowl quite satisfactorily for less than the cost of in-bowl cleaners.

Compared with liquids, powders are less convenient to apply around the bowl and under the rim.

The chemicals in toilet bowl cleaners are powerful and should be handled carefully. Never mix an in-bowl cleaner with other household chemicals (including in-tank toilet cleaners). To do so could release toxic fumes.

IN-TANK CLEANERS

Some in-tank products rely on blue dye to tint the water and hide the dirt that accumulates between scrubbings. Although blue cleaners generally contain detergent and other ingredients to curb stains, some do not actually claim to clean a dirty bowl. With some in-tank cleaners, then, the question is not how well it works but how long it lasts. Don't be too quick to change containers when the blue vanishes. Check to see if the dispensing valve has clogged or if the product is actually used up.

Some blue cleaners claim to deodorize. If you sniff packages on the store shelf, you may notice wintergreen, pine, or lemon scents. Indeed, the packages sometimes have a very strong smell. But once the cleaner dissolves in the tank, the scent may be practically imperceptible.

Some in-tank cleaners slowly dispense chlorine bleach to lighten stains and give off a scent that many people associate with cleanliness. These products may contain pebbles of calcium hypochlorite bleach.

The amount of bleach such cleaners release can vary considerably from flush to flush. Typically, it's very little. However, they release enough chlorine to bleach stains, since the water may stand in the bowl for hours. But when a toilet isn't flushed at least once a day, the bleach may become more concentrated and may damage parts inside the tank. Some plumbing-fixture manufacturers recommend against using in-tank cleaners containing hypochlorite bleach.

Since chlorine is not as visible as blue dye, you might not know when to replace a bleach-based bowl cleaner. If your water is chlorinated, your nose may not tell you. You can use a drop of food coloring in the bowl as a test. If the coloring lasts for more than a few minutes, it means that the bleach-based cleaner is spent.

RECOMMENDATIONS

The best way to clean the toilet bowl is to brush it frequently with a liquid all-purpose cleaner. In-bowl toilet cleaners are for more serious stains. Scrubbing with an acidic powder or liquid is the one sure way to attack the mineral matter that causes most toilet bowl stains, particularly around the rim.

In-tank cleaners, blue-colored or bleaches, are easy to use, but don't expect miracles. If you start with a spotless toilet, they may only slow the buildup of new stains and keep the bowl presentable between more thorough scrubbings. In-tank bleach cleaners should not be used in a toilet that isn't flushed regularly. Enough chlorine may accumulate to damage parts inside the tank.

Finally, do not let any brand's claims to disinfect sway you. At best, a disinfecting cleaner can only temporarily cut the population of some germs.

VACUUM CLEANERS

The two classic kinds of vacuum cleaner, upright and canister, have become more alike. Each has borrowed features from the other and become more versatile. Most upright vacuums now have a flexible hose and tools to vacuum crevices, upholstery, and furniture—tasks that were once the canister vacuum's alone. And, for carpet cleaning, many canisters now have a power nozzle—a smaller, detachable version of the upright's built-in power head. (Power heads and power nozzles use a rotating beater brush to deep-clean carpeting.)

Upright vacuums remain the most popular choice, outselling canister models by more than five to one. You should probably give first consideration to an upright vacuum. Among other advantages, it's likely to be easier to handle than a canister vacuum, and probably less expensive. A canister model might suit you if you vacuum mostly bare floors. The floor brush of a good canister vacuum may do a better job on flooring than the power head of an upright vacuum, whose brushes may disperse debris before it can be vacuumed up.

HOW THEY CLEANED

Nothing matters more in a vacuum cleaner, obviously, than how well it picks up dust and debris.

Carpet cleaning. Almost any vacuum cleaner can remove most surface debris. Better machines also pluck dirt from deep within carpet pile. Overall, there is little difference in deep-cleaning prowess between canisters and uprights. That wasn't the case in past years, when uprights held an edge.

Air flow. Most vacuum cleaners either pull or push debris-laden air through a porous vacuum bag that traps the waste. As the bag fills, air flow diminishes. This reduces the suction the machine can sustain. Canisters generally outdo uprights at the outset, but most of the canisters can't hold the edge as their bags fill.

For those times when a vacuum cleaner accidentally inhales part of a throw rug or drapes, it's handy to have a control that reduces suction—typically, a valve that uncovers a hole near the hose's handle. That allows you to pause, extract the fabric, and continue to vacuum, all without shutting off the machine. Most canister vacuums have such a suction control; most uprights don't.

CLEARING THE AIR

Even an excellent vacuum cleaner won't necessarily capture all dust and debris. Some of the waste gets blown around, and some is vented back into the room through the exhaust port. The particles most likely to escape filtration are minuscule, and can include fragments of such allergens as pet dander, pollen, and mold spores. A clean exhaust, then, is an important consideration to people who are sensitive to such substances.

The top performers are uprights whose suction fan is located in front of the vacuum bag and pushes air through the bag. That design does have a drawback, however: Because incoming air is drawn through the fan before it is filtered, there is a chance that a solid object—a coin, say—will damage the fan's vanes. Machines with that "push" fan design include all the "soft body" uprights, which enclose the bag in a fabric pouch, and some of the "hard body" uprights, which have a rigid plastic casing. The rest of the hard-body uprights and all of the canister vacuums are "pullers," with fans located downstream of the bag.

The vacuums that emit the most in their exhaust are canisters. However, even the dirtiest among them doesn't spew forth a visible torrent of debris. But the dust in their exhausts could irritate some people who are sensitive to airborne allergens. One option, available on about a third of the machines, is to use "microfiltration bags," which supposedly use electrostatic charges to trap small particles. If the vacuum cleaner allows a choice of bags, non-allergy sufferers should choose the standard-type bag; they're almost always less expensive than microfiltration bags.

WHAT'S EASIEST TO USE?

If you're a typical vacuum-cleaner owner, you'll live with your machine for years before it breaks. So you want to make sure the one you buy is as easy to use as possible. Here are some of the factors to consider:

Lugging it. You can usually hoist an upright with one hand. Canisters require both hands, not only because they're heavy, but also because you typically have to juggle more components at a time.

Getting started. Most vacuum cleaners have an On/Off switch that's easy to operate by hand or foot. A few force you to bend uncomfortably to reach the switch. Some canisters have a second, independent switch on or near the handle to control the power nozzle. That's a plus when an object gets stuck in the brush and you want to shut off the machine quickly.

Adjusting cleaning height. Deep cleaning goes better when the beater brushes are adjusted to the right height—too high and they won't clean deeply, too low and they'll dig into the pile and make the machine hard to push. Some machines claim to adjust the height automatically. Consumers Union favors machines that allow you to make the adjustment yourself, preferably using a foot pedal, and those models that allow the beater brush in the power head or nozzle to be switched off so that its rotation doesn't blow dirt around a bare floor.

Pushing and pulling. Once set at the proper height, most uprights are pretty easy to push, especially those with big wheels or rollers. Self-propelled models require little effort to push about. However, the power assistance does take getting used to. And, with the feature turned off, they may be difficult to move around.

Uprights require more effort to move about when the hose is in use than when they're deep cleaning. Some uprights have a hose that mounts high on the machine, making the vacuum prone to tip.

Stairs. On stairways, a canister vacuum is generally easier to use than an upright, whose wide "footprint" often won't fit comfortably on the stair. Vacuuming stairs is easier with a long hose, which enables you to cover most of the steps with the main unit at the bottom. You can do a more effective cleaning job on stairs and along baseboards if there's a minimum of dead space between the powered brush and the outer edge of its housing. Every power head or nozzle has such an area in front of and on each side of the housing.

Cord storage. A vacuum cleaner typically has a 20- to 30-foot power cord. Canisters usually have a handy built-in winder that automatically recoils the cord at the press of a button or a yank of the cord. Uprights typically have two hooks, around which you wind the cord. If one or both hooks swivel, the cord can be released quickly. However, some machines have awkward, annoying ways to store the cord. Others have no way at all to store it. **Whines and roars.** Canisters tend to be slightly less noisy than the uprights, and hard-body uprights less noisy than soft-body models.

Emptying dust and debris. To dispose of what a vacuum cleaner has picked up, you almost always have to change a paper bag. Uprights usually have the largest bags, but bags that are bigger don't necessarily last longer. Bags often must be replaced not because they're full, but because their pores have clogged, restricting air flow. Some machines have an indicator to let you know when the bag is full (or if air flow is blocked).

It's often awkward and sloppy to change bags on a soft-body upright. You may have to place the machine on its back, unzip the cloth pouch or remove a plastic retainer, and coax the bag's sleeve over a protruding tube. Removing the old bag without dumping debris is also a challenge, as is retrieving any spilled dirt from the bottom of the pouch.

MAINTAINING THE MACHINE

An object that's stuck in the revolving brush or fan blades can cause the motor to overheat and burn out. That's why some cleaners, mostly canisters, have a shutoff mechanism. Even if you escape such a calamity, vacuum cleaners still require occasional upkeep—replacing the brush, the drive belt, or the headlamp bulb are examples. Doing the upkeep yourself could not only save you a repair bill, which averages $40, but also the expense of needless repairs. Replacing parts yourself is easier on some machines than on others.

LIGHT VACUUMS FOR LIGHT DUTIES

No room to store a vacuum cleaner? Want some lightweight assistance with quick cleanups? The electric broom, which weighs about six pounds and usually costs less than $50, promises to help. An electric broom may be handy for quick (if a little dirty) once-overs on floors in, say, the kitchen or a small apartment. It may also be a boon for those with limited mobility or hand strength, who have trouble using either a full-size vacuum cleaner or a broom and dustpan.

WINDOW CLEANERS

Squeegee-wielding professionals know that plain water can clean lightly soiled windows. But if you put off washing your windows until they're really dirty, you'll need something more potent.

The best glass cleaner is one that works fast and removes grime with a minimum of help from you. Consumers Union's laboratory

NEWSPAPERS FOR CLEANING WINDOWS

Over the years, there have been many opinions about which window wipers work best. Professionals do their wiping with natural-sponge applicators and rubber squeegees. Some purists feel the job is unfinished without the careful application of a good chamois leather. Yet others swear by yesterday's newspaper.

In a Consumers Union test of newspaper used with an effective commercial cleaner on heavily soiled windows, it was found that newspaper is not very absorbent. It takes a fair amount of wiping and rubbing to clean and polish a window with it. Newspaper also blackens hands and leaves ink smudges around window mullions.

tests showed that glass cleaners widely vary in their effectiveness. Many are mediocre. Vinegar brands are generally inferior to ammonia-based versions.

HOMEMADE RECIPES

Consumers Union's recipes can equal or best many of the aerosols, sprays, and premoistened towels in the stores. They cost a fraction of the price for store-bought products—a penny or less per ounce—and you can easily prepare them at home.

■ *The Lemon Formula*—works for lightly soiled windows. Mix 4 tablespoons of lemon juice in 1 gallon of water.
■ *The Ammonia Formula*—works for heavily soiled windows. Mix ½ cup of sudsy ammonia, 1 pint of rubbing alcohol, and 1 tablespoon of hand dishwashing liquid (do not use more than 1 tablespoon, or streaking may result), and top the mixture up with enough water to make 1 gallon.

STORE PRODUCTS

A store-bought glass cleaner would cost from around a nickel to a quarter an ounce. Pump sprays generally carry a lower cost-per-ounce than do aerosols, and supermarket house brands are generally cheaper than national brands.

With most commercial products, an ounce of cleaner goes pretty far. It would cost on average only a few pennies to clean both sides of a heavily soiled window measuring 2 by 3 feet.

CARE IN USE

Any glass cleaner, even plain water, can soften latex paint on mullions and sills around a window. Therefore, wipe spilled window cleaner off painted surfaces without hard rubbing. The paint should reharden once it has dried.

THE ENVIRONMENT

Among the usual ingredients in most glass cleaners, none pose any problems for the environment. None of the cleaners contain phosphates, and none of the aerosols use ozone-depleting propellants.

Laundry

You can get good laundering results if you sort clothes according to the following guidelines:

- Separate colors and whites into different laundry loads. Intense colors (very dark or very bright) may bleed, especially when washed for the first time. They can tint white or light-colored clothes washed in the same load. A good guide is the maker's care label.
- Separate chlorine-bleachable light and white clothes from those that cannot be bleached if you intend to add chlorine bleach to the wash.
- Most wash loads do quite well in cold or warm water. Heavy soils on cottons respond better to a hot-water wash. Hot water may have an adverse effect on permanent-press garments. Check each garment's care label.
- Separate very dirty clothes that should be presoaked or washed in hot water from lightly soiled or temperature-sensitive items.
- Separate sweatshirts, new towels, and products made from chenille yarn (all of which may tend to generate lint) from permanent press clothes and corduroys (which attract lint).
- As you sort wash loads, remember to empty pockets and close zippers to prevent snagging. Next, check for troublesome stains that may have become set. Some stains won't respond well to

a presoak or laundry booster alone, and require special treatment before washing. Check Appendix B: Stain Removal for detailed instructions on removing those stains.

■ To keep socks from getting lost, place them at the bottom of the washing machine tub, wash them in a mesh bag, or use "sock savers," plastic rings designed to lock pairs of socks together.

■ Do not overload your dryer. Always allow ample room for articles to tumble about freely. Placing too many items in a dryer can lengthen drying time and cause garments to wrinkle. Leaving clothes in the dryer's drum after tumbling has stopped can also cause wrinkling.

■ To ensure optimum drying time, be sure to clean the dryer's lint filter after each use.

For the best ways to cope with laundry, check the following sections on Bleaches, Boosters, Clothes Washers, Detergents, and Fabric Softeners.

BLEACHES

Liquid chlorine bleach is the old standby, having earned its place in the laundry room, bathroom, and kitchen for whitening and removing stains and mildew. But chlorine bleach has its problems, too. The telltale signs of misuse or overuse of chlorine bleach are splotches of faded color or white spots where undiluted bleach has splashed, and fabrics that have faded from vivid to dim or from blue to pink.

Nonchlorine, "all-fabric" oxygen bleaches promise the benefits of chlorine bleach without the risk. However, the real story unfolds in the laundry room.

Chlorine and oxygen bleaches use different active ingredients that decolorize and solubilize stains so they can be removed with the help of a detergent. Liquid chlorine bleaches all have about the same amount of active ingredient, sodium hypochlorite, and there is little difference from one brand to another. The active ingredient in liquid oxygen bleaches is hydrogen peroxide. In powder oxygen bleaches it is sodium percarbonate or sodium perborate tetrahydrate. Oxygen bleaches usually contain other ingredients as well to help in stain removal.

Chlorine bleaches have always been far better than oxygen bleaches at whitening clothes. Oxygen bleaches can only maintain whiteness, not restore it.

HARD-TO-REMOVE STAINS

In general, chlorine or oxygen bleach should be used with a good laundry detergent to succeed at removing stains. Some oxygen bleaches are better than chlorine bleaches at reducing or removing tough stains such as red wine.

FADING

Chlorine bleach can cause colors to fade. Initially, it may have no noticeable effect on the brightness of colors. After a few washings, however, the chlorine begins taking its toll. Slight fading becomes evident and then, after more washings, objectionable. An oxygen bleach will continue being kind to colors much longer.

RECOMMENDATIONS

Chlorine bleach, when used properly, is the most effective way to whiten fabrics, including some synthetics. It's ideal for the occasional whitening your wash may need, but knowing how to use chlorine bleach is essential: Improper and long-term use may take its toll on colors and fabric life. Using chlorine bleach may be tricky, but buying it is simple. The only real difference you are likely to find is price.

All-fabric oxygen bleaches have the advantage of being safe with most fabrics and dyes, even over the long term. But they're much more expensive to use than chlorine bleaches.

A good approach is the occasional use of chlorine bleach on chlorine-safe white fabrics to deliver the whitening you need. Never use chlorine and oxygen bleaches together; they will counteract each other. Use all-fabric bleach to brighten colors without fading and to whiten fabrics that are not safe for use with chlorine bleach.

When you use bleach, follow these guidelines:

■ Before you bleach, read the garment's care label. If it says "no bleach," don't use any kind of bleach. Chlorine bleach is usually safe on cottons, linens, and some colorfast fabrics.

■ Don't use chlorine bleach on wool, silk, mohair, leather (e.g., buttons, Spandex, or noncolorfast fabrics or dyes). If you're unsure about the safety of a bleach for a garment, first do a safety test on an inside seam as recommended on the bleach's label.

■ *Never* use chlorine bleach with hand dishwashing liquids, ammonia, or toilet cleaners. The combination can produce irritating fumes.

■ Chlorine bleach must first be diluted as directed on the product's label. It should then be added 5 to 6 minutes after the wash cycle has started.

■ Oxygen bleach should be added with the laundry detergent to the wash water before the laundry is added. It is safe on washable fabrics. It works more effectively at higher wash temperatures than at cooler temperatures.

BOOSTERS

Today's high-performance laundry detergents do not need a laundry booster to remove many common stains. However, some household stains, such as used motor oil, are too stubborn for some laundry detergents in ordinary laundering. Stain-fighting laundry boosters may help a laundry detergent to remove stubborn stains.

Boosters may be available as powders, pump sprays, aerosols, liquids, and sticks. Regular laundry detergents can also be used as self-boosters. Liquid laundry detergents are effective stain removers when applied directly to stains before laundering. Powder laundry detergents should be mixed with a little water and applied to the stain as a paste—rubbed in with a new, soft toothbrush— before laundering.

Consumers Union tested the effectiveness of boosters and liquid laundry detergents on eleven different stains on white cotton-polyester fabric: chocolate syrup, makeup, grape juice, spaghetti sauce, blood, mud, grass, tea, black ink, and used motor oil. Boosters were used according to label instructions to help an economy-priced laundry detergent, but without presoaking. Performance was spotty and disappointing in general. The best boosters were effective on four to six of the eleven stains; the other boosters on only one or two. One booster was not effective at removing any of the stains.

CONVENIENCE

Launderers with a single-stained garment might like a stick. But there are situations in which a stick would be decidedly inconvenient. Imagine rubbing a wash load of grass-stained knees, oil-stained overalls, and T-shirts dotted with last week's spaghetti dinner. Liquids, likewise, must be rubbed in. Sprays are a bit easier; you douse stains, then toss the dirty clothes into the washing machine. When stains are pervasive, you might prefer a powder that you pour into the machine along with a detergent. But presoaking with a powder is problematic. You can let the stained clothes soak in the water, but that ties up the machine. A messy alternative is to let the laundry soak in a tub, then transfer it to your washing machine.

RECOMMENDATIONS

Laundry detergents are generally so effective that you may not need a booster if you lead a low-soil life. You can also use the detergent as a booster as described above. It may make sense, however, to keep a booster on hand for those inevitable spills that even the best detergent can't handle. Choose a product based on your idea of convenience. Some boosters cope quite well with some stains, but most aren't any more effective than detergent alone.

MAIL-ORDER BOOSTER/SPOT REMOVERS

Consumers Union conducted tests on two specialized spot removers, *Amodex Stain Remover* (Amodex Products, Inc., P.O. Box 3332, 989 Hancock Avenue, Bridgeport, CT 06065) and *Magic Wand* (Edwards Creative Products, P.O. Box 8361, Cherry Hill, NJ 08002). Both performed better, overall, than supermarket boosters. But they weren't equally effective on all stains. *Amodex* was better as both a prespotter and spot remover, removing more stains from more fabrics.

CLOTHES WASHERS

The design of top-loading automatic washing machines has matured to the point that periodic model changes are mostly small refinements. A manufacturer may change the shape of the agitator, or restyle the control panel, or replace mechanical controls with electronic ones.

Except for lower-end models, most machines come with such amenities as two agitation and spin speeds, variable water-level controls, and bleach and fabric-softener dispensers. Less expensive models may have somewhat smaller capacities and lack some of those features or have less elaborate versions of them. Most of the rather deluxe washers have mechanical controls; several models have electronic controls. "Suds saver" models, of which very few are manufactured, let users recycle the wash water.

Almost all washing machines sold in the United States are top-loaders, with wash tubs that rotate around a vertical axis. While front-loading washers, with wash tubs that rotate around a horizontal axis, are available, very few are sold in the United States. This is the case even though front-loaders use much less water, energy (mainly in the form of hot water used for washing), and detergent. However, manufacturers expect that within the near future, DOE energy standards will be much more stringent, and the most practical way to meet the standard will be with horizontal axis washers. While all horizontal axis machines presently sold in the United States are front-loaders, future horizontal axis machines may be designed to be loaded from the top. Models of that design are available in Europe. Present front-loaders sell for $600 to well over $1,000. Whether the new horizontal axis machines will be sold for as low a price as present top-loaders remains to be seen.

Just about any washing machine on the market will clean just fine, provided you use the right cycle, the right amount of detergent, and the right amount of water. Other critical factors are convenience, efficiency (machines that use less water get higher marks), and load-size capacity.

For a machine to wash properly, clothes must move around the tub, toward the agitator, then sink. If that doesn't happen, the clothes nearest the agitator take a pounding while those around the side move only slightly.

Consumers Union's testers made up loads of white or light-colored items plus six "flags"—brightly colored washcloths. The testers put each machine through its regular cycle with the lid up so they could count and time the appearance and disappearance of the flags. If the flags circulated well, the testers ran larger loads until two flags no longer circulated.

These tests showed considerable differences in capacity. The size and shape of the tub, the design of the agitator, agitator speed, and time contribute heavily to those differences.

ENERGY AND WATER

Water consumption is a critical factor, given the periodic drought in some parts of the country, the strain that a large load of wash water imposes on septic systems, and the cost of heating the wash water. (Providing hot water consumes far more energy than running the washing machine itself.) To monitor water and energy consumption, tests were run using the warm wash/cold rinse settings that are suitable for most clothes.

Water use. On a regular cycle with an eight-pound load, water use ranged from about 40 to 50 gallons. On the permanent-press cycle, consumption was slightly more. Front-loaders used about one-half to one-third of the water used by top-loaders.

Washers are most efficient when run at full capacity, using the highest water level. You can adjust the water level for partial loads, but you shouldn't try to wash a full load on a partial water fill. That will hamper the machine's performance and may also damage the clothing.

Energy use. The range of hot-water use for the machines is striking. Assume you do about 42 pounds of clothes per week, or 2,184 pounds per year. One of the more efficient machines would do that much laundry in about 160 loads, using 1,800 gallons of hot water per year. A relatively inefficient machine would need about 240 loads and 2,800 gallons of hot water. That's about 45 percent more. Actual differences would probably be less dramatic because you wouldn't fill a machine to capacity for every load.

The "suds saver." One "suds-saver" machine design, which should more accurately be termed a water saver, spews wash water into a tub or sink next to the machine, then sucks it up again to be reused for one or more additional wash-water fills. Sediment from the first wash settles out in the sink or tub. The washer's intake hose is designed to leave about half an inch of water, so the sediment is not pumped back. That arrangement saves about 17 gallons of water and about half the detergent for

---

REPAIR HISTORY

Washing machines from KitchenAid, Whirlpool, and Hotpoint have had a more reliable record than other brands, according to a 1994 *Consumer Reports* reader survey. Machines from White-Westinghouse, Frigidaire, and Magic Chef have been the most trouble-prone.

The older the washer, of course, the more likely it has ever been repaired. Accordingly, age is taken into account when analyzing the repair data. Usage also affects a washer's reliability. Among machines used for one to four loads a week, only 15 percent ever needed repair. Some 20 percent of the machines used for five to seven loads a week have needed some repair. And 26 percent of the machines used for eight or more loads per week have needed repair.

each reuse. About a gallon of fresh water is added to the next load of laundry to compensate for what was left in the sink. The more the wash water is reused, the cooler and the less effective it becomes; it is up to the user to decide when to stop recycling. Fresh detergent in each reuse, plus fresh-water rinses, keep cleaning performance up.

OTHER CHARACTERISTICS

Here are some aspects of performance other than capacity and efficiency.

Unbalanced loads. Ski jackets, mattress pads, blankets, and other bulky items strain a machine's suspension by making the tub oscillate as it spins. Consumers Union's testers gave each machine an increasingly unbalanced load and watched to see if the machine banged or "walked" across the floor. A few machines did quite well. Others banged loudly even with a moderately unbalanced load. Some machines have a switch that shuts the machine off if the load goes out of balance. But such a switch can work all too well, sometimes shutting off the machines with even a slightly unbalanced load.

To minimize rocking and vibration, the legs on a washer must be set so that the machine is level yet kept as close to the floor as possible. Many machines have self-leveling rear legs linked together, a design that makes the machine easier to level.

Sand disposal. Most machines do quite well in removing fairly large amounts of sand in the first wash. Even the worst should remove all the sand after two washes.

Linting. Laundering inevitably produces lint, but a well-designed washing machine should filter it out. Most even have a self-cleaning lint filter that flushes lint away when spinning.

Noise. Noise becomes an important consideration if you live in an apartment or a house where the washer is near the main living area. As a rule, machines are quietest in the Spin cycle, noisiest when filling with water. Although the Fill cycle is short, it can be downright boisterous.

Safety. Most machines on the market are designed to minimize hazards. The majority have a brake that stops the spinning tub if you lift the lid. Some lock the lid during Spin and make it impossible to lift the lid for about 45 seconds after the tub has stopped.

CONTROL

Most washers on the market let you choose a Regular cycle, a Permanent Press cycle (with an extra cold-water spray or a deep rinse to relax wrinkles), and a Knits/Delicates cycle (with slow agitation and spin). Some models with mechanical controls show only Regular and Permanent Press cycles, but they allow you to control agitation and spin speeds. Other machines automatically set agitation and spin speeds when you choose a cycle.

Many machines offer a setting for a second rinse, but any of these machines can be set by hand for an additional rinse and spin at the end of a cycle. An extra rinse is useful if you're using extra detergent to wash heavily soiled items or if you're sensitive to detergent and want to be sure it's removed from the clothes. Otherwise, the extra rinse just wastes water.

Most machines can be set for at least the basic wash and rinse temperatures: a hot wash/cold rinse for white or very soiled colorfast items; a warm wash/cold rinse for more lightly soiled or permanent press items; and a cold wash/cold rinse for delicates.

A few have additional water-temperature settings between hot and warm and warm and cold. They provide more flexibility in adapting choice to specific water temperatures. Other washing machines offer warm wash/warm rinse and slow agitation, settings that are preferable for washable woolens.

A few models have an electronic temperature control. It's supposed to regulate the mix of hot and cold to produce warm water. Other machines mix a preset proportion of cold and hot.

Manual controls differ in their ease of use. Large, easy-to-read lettering, uncluttered areas and color, or other clear markers to illustrate the different cycles are best. No dial has it all. But some are straightforward and color-coded. Others have very large, easy-to-read dials that may be better suited for visually impaired persons.

An electronically controlled machine may seem formidable at first, but most prove simple to use. With the typical electronic machine, you choose a cycle, then press Start. The electronics handle all the choices for water temperature, agitation, and the like. You can use Up/Down buttons to change the preset water level, the water temperature, the washing time, and so on. Some machines display prompts to show you which button needs to be pressed next.

Electronically controlled units usually command a premium price. A retired independent repairman told Consumers Union that electronic controls are more expensive to repair than mechanical ones. But the manufacturers Consumers Union contacted maintained that electronic controls in washing machines are inherently more reliable than mechanical ones. Any problems that occur show up immediately and can be fixed under warranty, say the manufacturers.

RECOMMENDATIONS

Deluxe machines come with the added features and price tags that typify top-of-the-line equipment. Less-expensive machines should get your clothes just as clean, but they may have a smaller tub or more rudimentary controls. They may also lack such amenities as a bleach or fabric-softener dispenser.

Models with conventional manual controls seem to offer better value. The electronic machines perform no better overall, and they sell for $100 to $300 more than their mechanical counterparts.

Detergents

Detergent manufacturers try to attract buyers with specific laundry problems. There are powders and liquids that ease pretreatment of tough soils. Some detergents come with special ingredients such as color-safe bleach, fabric softener, or stain-fighting enzymes. Some are free of perfumes and dyes. Practically all are made without phosphates to avoid possible harm to waterways. Several "green" brands suggest that they will give the user not only a cleaner clean but a healthier planet.

There are only a few remaining regular-strength detergents. Most now come in concentrated strengths. And now there are superconcentrated or "ultra" products, whose containers are as small as a lunch box but can hold enough detergent for many loads.

The truth is that all detergents clean lightly soiled clothes. But some are better than others at keeping loosened soil from settling back on clothes, for stain removal, and in brightening. Powders, as a class, outperform most liquids. Major national brands of powders and liquids perform better than store brands. Products that contain bleach or "bleach alternative" tend to outperform those that do not. Some mail-order and health-food store "green brands" do not perform as well as some regular store brands. They also may cost more.

STAIN REMOVAL

No laundry detergent will completely remove all common stains. But most major national brands of powders—especially those with bleach or bleach alternative—can remove many common stains better than most liquids. Laundry detergents at best are only fair at removing used motor-oil stains. However, results improve remarkably if you use certain detergent boosters before laundering.

BRIGHTENING

Most laundry detergents contain ingredients that absorb ultraviolet light from the sun or from fluorescent fixtures and emit it as blue light. Even laundry detergents that claim to be free of perfumes and dyes can contain brighteners. Most powders produce a brighter blue-white glow than most liquids.

COSTS

The cost per six-pound load of heavily soiled clothes laundered in moderately hard warm water averages about 30 to 40 cents. However, the full range of costs is rather wide for regular liquids, from 23 to 52 cents. For major concentrated liquids the range is from 16 to 69 cents per load. For super-concentrated powders the cost is from 13 to 64 cents.

RECOMMENDATIONS

If your laundry rarely has stubborn stains, buy by price. You can save the most money by forgetting brand loyalty: Clip coupons and stock up on whatever satisfactory product is on sale.

If you regularly wash heavily stained clothes, choose a powder rather than a liquid and a major brand rather than a store brand. Select the lowest-price major brand rather than a higher-price one. The differences in performance will be small.

DETERGENT INGREDIENTS

Here's a rundown of five key ingredients you might find on a package of laundry detergent.

Surfactants, or surface active agents, are dirt removers. They emulsify, suspend, and disperse oil, grease, and dirt, allowing all of that to be washed away. There are many such chemicals, and detergents may contain more than one kind. *Anionic* surfactants, which have a negative electrical charge, work best in warm, soft water. They are very effective on oily stains and in removing clay. *Nonionic* surfactants, which lack an electrical charge, are less sensitive to water hardness. They excel at removing oily soils. Many detergents contain this type. Some powders and liquids contain both anionic and nonionic surfactants. *Cationic* surfactants, which carry a positive charge, are more common in fabric softeners.

Builders enhance the cleaning efficiency of surfactants by softening the water. Some also maintain a desirable level of alkalinity, which boosts cleaning. Phosphates are builders. They have been replaced by other builders such as zeolites. Some powders use washing soda with extra ingredients to make up for the lack of phosphorus. Liquids may contain other water-softening chemicals such as sodium citrate.

Whitening agents, also known as fluorescent brighteners, give laundry an added blue glow in sunlight and fluorescent light, making garments appear brighter than they otherwise would.

Enzymes help break down complex soils so they can be more easily removed. Two common types of enzymes are protease and amylase. A protease breaks down protein, as in egg or bloodstains. An amylase digests carbohydrates, as in honey or maple syrup.

All-fabric bleach is an addition to some detergent powders. All-fabric bleaches, sodium percarbonate or sodium perborate tetrahydrate, are safe on most colored washable fabrics except those with a care label warning "no bleach."

DETERGENTS AND THE ENVIRONMENT

The washing machine or dishwasher completes its cycle; you pull out the clean clothes or dishes; the wash water has drained away—somewhere. After you've finished using a detergent product, you throw away the empty carton, box, bottle, or can. It goes into a garbage truck and is driven away—somewhere. But what happens to that water and those containers? Here is a primer on the environmental ramifications of cleaning.

Biodegradable? Many detergent products claim to be biodegradable or to contain biodegradable ingredients. The fact is that all surfactants (the main cleaning agents) in today's cleaning products are biodegradable and are quickly and thoroughly broken down during wastewater treatment.

Some manufacturers promote their "natural ingredient" products as being better for the environment than those made with synthetic (petroleum-derived) ingredients. They state that their respective vegetable-based surfactants are for people who care about the environment, and that their products save petroleum, a limited natural resource.

Petroleum-derived oils and vegetable-derived oils are used as feed stocks for many detergent surfactants. Both types come from "natural" sources. In each case, the oils are chemically processed to make the surfactants. They are, therefore, all "synthetic."

Although there are environmental impacts associated with the manufacture of either vegetable *or* petroleum-derived surfactants, there is no inherent environmental advantage to using one surfactant source over the other. Minor ingredients such as optical brighteners and fragrances may degrade less rapidly than other ingredients, but Consumers Union has seen no convincing evidence that they cause any harm. Overall, detergents are pretty benign to the environment. Without conducting a complex and exceedingly difficult life-cycle analysis, it is not possible to compare overall environmental costs of different detergent products. Accordingly, any claimed advantages of the "green" brands should be taken with a grain of salt and weighed against product performance and cost.

Phosphates. Some liquid detergent products' labels say they are phosphate-free; others don't. But phosphates aren't soluble or stable enough to be used in liquid detergents. Accordingly, all are phosphate-free.

Phosphated detergents, blamed for contributing to the growth of algae in waterways, have been banned in many regions of the country. Now, most national powder laundry detergent products are also phosphate-free. Most detergents formulated for use in dishwashers—powder and gel—contain phosphates.

Packaging. A few years ago, plastic containers seemed an environmental evil; the package of choice was made of paper or cardboard. Paper is "biodegradable," the thinking went, and eventually returns to the soil. But when it's in a landfill devoid of light and air, paper has staying power. In 1989, garbage archaeologists unearthed readable newspapers from 1942. It's clear that once trash (or at least nontoxic trash) lands in a landfill, its composition matters less than its volume.

As landfills, the final resting place for most of America's garbage, fill up and close down, packaging may become a more important reason for selecting or rejecting a product. Some laundry packages lining store shelves contain recycled materials. Cardboard boxes always have; many plastic bottles do now, too.

Recycling differs from community to community. Although plastic bottles and paperboard boxes may be labeled *recyclable*, they aren't always *recycled*. Most recycling programs take high-density polyethylene bottles. Paperboard cartons, although theoretically recyclable, fall into a category of "mixed paper," which is rarely included in curbside recycling programs because there's not much of a market for it.

Refills for superconcentrated laundry detergents often come in containers that make use of less material than their original, reusable packaging. The same is essentially true in the case of most liquid laundry detergents. Differences in the amount of waste are a function of the detergents' cleaning ability rather than the size of their packages. A concentrated detergent that cleans 20 washer loads with three pounds of powder leaves behind far less packaging than a six-pound package that cleans the same number of loads. Many ultraconcentrated detergents excel in this regard.

DRY CLEANING

Dry cleaning launders clothes in a solvent, often with detergent and sometimes a little water. It is recommended for materials such as wool, which might shrink and suffer other damage if laundered with conventional detergent and water. Currently, the great majority of dry-cleaning establishments use the solvent perchloroethylene for general dry cleaning. For spot removal, the choice of solvent depends on the type of spot and the fabric.

Use of perchloroethylene raises certain environmental and human health concerns. The solvent is present in low levels in the atmosphere in cities. It is released slowly from fabrics, so bringing home and wearing dry-cleaned clothes exposes the consumer to perchloroethylene.

Perchloroethylene is classed as a possible human carcinogen by the U.S. Environmental Protection Agency (EPA) and is being re-classified by the International Agency for Research on Cancer (IARC) as a likely human carcinogen. Over time, even low doses of perchloroethylene may increase risk of cancer. People exposed to moderate doses of perchloroethylene for a long time have experienced kidney damage and altered liver function, as well as altered neurological function.

The best way for most people to minimize exposure to perchloroethylene is to minimize the amount of dry cleaning they do. Don't dry clean a garment that doesn't need it. A suit that's wrinkled or baggy may need only to be pressed. If you brush a suit after each wearing, it can go a long time between cleanings, barring a stain. With clothes other than suits and sports jackets, try hand washing and ironing rather than dry cleaning. Many fabrics, including silk and rayon, usually do fine in detergent and water, if handled with care.

Don't store newly dry cleaned clothes in a child's room. Since children are smaller than adults, they're more sensitive to toxins.

If possible, wait a week or more to let the solvent dissipate before using newly dry cleaned items. A dry-cleaning establishment should remove as much cleaning agent as possible before delivering a garment to you. If you detect a residual chemical odor, return it to the store for further processing or look for another shop.

Because of the environmental and health problems from dry-cleaning solvents, alternative "multiprocess wet cleaning" facilities are becoming franchised in several cities. In this aqueous cleaning process, the cleaner selects among various cleaning techniques (including steam cleaning, spot removing, hand washing, gentle machine washing, tumble drying, and vacuuming) to ensure that garments made of different fabrics are cleaned—hopefully—without damage. In 1993 the EPA published a report on a study designed to compare multiprocess wet cleaning with dry cleaning. Although there isn't enough data to determine if the method can be used to clean all materials safely, the EPA concluded that it is a viable option to reduce the usage of dry-cleaning solvents. If there is an outlet near you, consider trying it.

FABRIC SOFTENERS

Detergents can wash fibers so thoroughly that they leave clothes feeling scratchy; dryers can cause clothes to cling to each other because of buildup of static charge. (This is especially true with synthetic fabrics.)

Fabric softeners are waxy materials that are related to soap. They work by coating your laundry with waxy lubricants and humectant chemicals. The lubricants let fibers slide past each other, reducing wrinkling. They also separate a napped fabric's fibers and stand them on end, which makes a towel, for instance, feel fluffy. The humectants help the fabric retain moisture to dissipate the static charges that would otherwise cause clothes to cling and sparks to fly when you pull them apart. Many people use a fabric softener to cut static cling caused by the dryer's tumbling. The friction-reducing chemicals in softeners prevent a static charge from accumulating.

There are three basic types of fabric softeners. *Rinse liquids* are added to the wash during the rinse cycle; many washing machines automatically add them from a dispenser atop the agitator. *Dryer sheets* are impregnated with softener. When you put a sheet into the dryer along with the laundry, contact and heat release the softener. *Detergents with fabric softeners* are added at the start of the wash cycle.

For best results, add rinse liquids at the beginning of the final rinse (after a wash with a regular laundry detergent that does not contain softener). Place dryer sheets on top of the wet laundry to help prevent spotting.

The most effective softeners are the rinse liquids, but the least effective rinse liquids perform much more poorly than the best. Major brands and store brands of dryer sheets soften to roughly the same degree; about as effectively as average-performing rinse liquids. Detergents that contain softeners are mediocre at softening as well as cleaning.

Other Considerations

Brightening. The waxy coating left by fabric softeners may eventually make clothes look dingy. If whiter whites and brighter brights are important to you, use a high-performing laundry detergent with high brightening ability before you add a fabric softener.

Fragrance. Makers of laundry detergents include fragrances partly because some consumers like them and partly to hide the smell of other chemical ingredients. No matter how potent it seems in the package, the fragrance is muted considerably by the time the wash is done. If you like a fabric softener for its other qualities but dislike the smell, let your clothes air out for a while before you put them away. Some people can't tolerate any fragrance, whether for aesthetic or medical reasons. Fabric softeners and laundry detergents that are perfume-free are available.

Pricing

The cost per use of rinse liquids tends to be higher than that of dryer sheets. Detergents that contain fabric softeners are not money-saving products; they neither clean nor soften as well as single-purpose products. You can save money by buying whatever is on sale or using cents-off coupons.

HAND-LAUNDRY DETERGENTS

Your best guide on how to clean a fabric is the care label, which by law must be sewn into all articles of clothing. If the label says a garment must be dry-cleaned, follow that advice, or you will have no recourse with the manufacturer or retailer should something go wrong. If the label permits hand washing, you have to decide how to wash it.

On the supermarket shelves, next to the regular laundry detergents, you may find several products that make special claims for laundering fine washables of such fabrics as linen, wool, cotton, and silk. Many hand dishwashing liquids also say they can be used to launder fine washables.

WASHING WITH DETERGENT

Detergents are a big improvement over old-fashioned soap. In hard water, soaps leave behind a gray scum if you don't rinse well. Not so with detergents; they have ingredients to lift off soil and keep it suspended in the wash water. Detergents generally include other ingredients to help remove grease and other soils. Some have optical brighteners to make whites look whiter and enzymes to help attack stains.

EFFECTIVENESS

For safe and effective hand laundering of fine washables, try very gentle hand washing at 70ºF, a temperature warm enough to be comfortable to hands but cool enough to prevent shrinkage. Keep wash and rinse times to a few minutes each. The less time delicate fabrics are left soaking, the better.

The optical brighteners found in some hand-laundering products adhere to fabric and give off a bluish color in sunlight or under fluorescent lights, which makes white cloth appear whiter than it really is. Brighteners tend to work best on cotton.

HANDLE WITH CARE

Heat causes shrinkage, which is why fine fabrics are typically labeled for cold or cool wash, with no drying in the dryer. Silk crepe tends to pucker and requires ironing after washing. Rayon washes poorly; it wrinkles badly unless pressed while quite damp. Wool crepe, its weave tighter in one direction, can lose shape. If, before washing, a fabric has more "give" in one direction as you gently stretch it, you may have shrinkage problems.

When you hand-wash garments, roll them between towels and let them dry flat, away from heat and sunlight; do not wring them. It's prudent not to launder wool or silk in any enzyme-containing detergent unless the product's label says it's safe for them.

RECOMMENDATIONS

There is no reason to buy one of the specialized brands of detergents. Use a hand dishwashing liquid. All it lacks is the optical brightener that regular detergents and most hand-wash products contain to give whites extra dazzle. At about a penny a wash, hand dishwashing liquids are bargains. Even if you have stains to clean, you may have some luck with dishwashing liquid, depending on the fiber and type of stain.

Metal
Maintenance

METAL POLISHES

Although many metal polishes make broad claims, no one product is likely to be labeled for use on all of the following: silver, brass, copper, stainless steel, aluminum, and chrome.

COPPER AND BRASS

Copper and brass can be cleaned with a commercial cleaner available in your supermarket. Some of these products must be washed off thoroughly, because they can stain or etch metals if left in contact with them. Others, however, may be wiped or rubbed off. It is a good idea, therefore, to restrict your choice to a wipe-off polish for objects that can't be readily rinsed or submersed.

Some wipe-off brands may produce a better shine. Wash-off products, however, require less elbow grease to remove tarnish than do polishes of the wipe-off variety—a difference that you might consider important if you have to clean a heavily tarnished surface.

For objects that may be only thinly coated with brass or copper, you should use the mildest cleaning method possible. This means a cloth with hand dishwashing liquid and water.

Before any polish can work, the metal surface must be free of any lacquer. Of course, it may or may not have a lacquer. If it does, clean it but don't attempt to polish it.

COPPER-BOTTOMED COOKWARE

Wash-off polishes are particularly well suited to cookware, which can be easily washed and doesn't require a high gloss. These products should be able to remove light tarnish with little or no rubbing and heavy tarnish with less effort than a wipe-off material. Even with the most efficient product, you still must use considerable elbow grease to clean a heavily blackened pan bottom, and still the metal polish may not work. Steel wool will do the job more easily than polish but may leave the copper surface scratched and its mirrorlike finish diminished. If your pans are in bad shape but you are display conscious, you might first scour off the worst of the dirt with very fine steel wool and then finish the job with a wipe-off polish. This will avoid scratch marks and result in a good gloss.

SAFETY

Polishes, like other household chemicals, should be kept out of the reach of children. Some products carry special warnings.

HOW TO POLISH STAINLESS STEEL, ALUMINUM, AND CHROME

Stainless steel may stain with heat; aluminum becomes discolored with use, and its polished surface may dull; chrome doesn't tarnish, but it can become dirty and splotched.

Stainless steel. Ordinary cleaning in the sink will suffice for stainless-steel cookware except for an occasional stain from heat.

To remove heat stains from the matte finish inside of a saucepan or fry pan, a commercial stainless steel cleaner can do a competent job, at least as good as and maybe better than soapy steel wool. If the pan's polished exterior is also stained, use a polishing product cautiously. Work as quickly as possible to avoid leaving chemicals in contact with the metal for any length of time, and be sure to rinse thoroughly.

Aluminum. You shouldn't expect to be able to restore a polished aluminum finish to its original glossiness. Soapy steel wool will probably restore some of the luster. Rubbing the metal in a straight back-and-forth motion, rather than in circles, helps to maintain a uniform appearance.

Chrome. The chrome plating on a metal product may be so thin that it is best not to use any abrasive polish on it at all. The mildest cleaning method possible should be used for chrome-plated appliances and utensils.

CLEANING OTHER COOKWARE TYPES

Cast iron. Wash cast-iron cookware in hot water and hand dishwashing liquid, but do not scour. Rinse and dry the cookware immediately after cleaning to avoid rusting. If manufacturer's instructions recommend oiling, do so after cleaning.

Enameled cookware. Clean enameled cookware in warm sudsy water. Soak pots to loosen burned-on foods and to remove stubborn stains. If necessary, use a nonabrasive cleanser and a nonabrasive scrubbing pad. Cookware that has a nonstick finish can be cleaned in the dishwasher.

SILVER CARE

One type of silver-care product (three-way) removes tarnish, polishes, and treats silver with chemicals that retard further tarnishing. Another variety (two-way) cleans and polishes but doesn't claim to retard tarnishing. Both types of products include a mild abrasive. You rub on the polish, wipe it off, and then buff the finish to the shine you want.

There are also one-way products that come in liquid form and are used for cleaning only. They don't require tedious rubbing to remove tarnish. You just dip the silver in them or spread them onto silver surfaces. Acidic dip cleaners, as a class, have some inherent hazards: Wear plastic or rubber gloves to protect your hands while cleaning, because contact with the cleaner may irritate skin. Be careful not to get any cleaner in your eyes. Since excessive inhalation of their sulfide fumes may be disagreeable and may cause headaches, these cleaners should be used only where there is good ventilation. Rinse silver thoroughly after cleaning with acidic dip products.

Using Jeweler's Rouge

Cleaning and polishing heavily tarnished silver with a stick of jeweler's rouge entails coating a piece of flannel with rouge, rubbing silver surfaces with the flannel until they are tarnish-free, then buffing the silver with a piece of clean flannel. The result will be silver just about as clean and bright as you can get with the best silver polish. This method has two drawbacks: You have to rub a lot more, and the process is messy, producing quantities of red particles that can smudge clothes and furnishings and can accumulate in the details, requiring scrubbing with a soft brush to remove. Rouge, however, is much cheaper than regular polish, and the cloths you use for cleaning are reusable until they start to come apart. You can get rouge from hobby shops or firms that supply professional jewelers. Look in the Yellow Pages under "Jewelers' Supplies" and "Craft Supplies."

Special Problems

Antique finishes. Dark-looking silver with an antique or oxidized finish is often deeply patterned. Silver polish is almost certain to remove some of the finish. Dip cleansers damage antique finishes, too, even when you carefully wipe the liquids onto the silver.

Satin finishes. Dips remove tarnish from satin, or low-luster, finishes without making them shinier (to some degree).

Staining. If you accidentally allow drops of polish to fall on silver pieces, dip cleaners may leave pale stains. You have to repolish to remove the stains. Many silver table knives are made with stainless steel blades, and—just as the label warns—drops from dip cleaners can permanently spot or even pit stainless steel if allowed to dry on the surface. To avoid damage, rinse such knives promptly after using a dip cleaner on their silver handles.

Recommendations

As a class, three-way products may be higher priced than other products. Nonetheless, a good three-way product is preferred. It also does the job of polishing—and does it well. What's more, because of its tarnish retardance, you won't have to clean the silver again quite as soon as you would with other polishes. Dip cleaners work fast, but you may still need to use a polish afterward, and polishing, after all, is like cleaning all over again.

Miscellaneous

AIR CLEANERS

A house can harbor a wide variety of pollutants: radon gas, cigarette smoke, cooking fumes; gases and smoke from furnaces and gas ranges; solvents from dry-cleaned clothing; and chemicals from paints, household cleaners, bug sprays, and the like. In the average American house, outdoor air replaces indoor air at the rate of only about one air change an hour. A "tight" house, with well-sealed windows and doors, may have an air exchange only once every four or five hours.

Obviously, you can ventilate the house by opening the windows, especially when cooking or painting. But you wouldn't want to do that when the weather is very hot or cold. Obviously, too, the more pollutants and irritants you can eliminate or control, the better. You can keep dust mites at bay, for example, if you wash bedding in hot water. And a kitchen exhaust fan can control cooking odors and smoke.

Using an appliance to clear the air can be less effective, and much more expensive, than opening a window. Most air cleaners are designed to remove smoke and dust but not gases, tobacco

111

odors, or viruses and bacteria. And an air cleaner can never completely eliminate pollution; new contaminants enter the house constantly.

A typical tabletop air cleaner can move only small amounts of air each minute; it is suitable for a small room or part of a large room. Bigger models are designed to move several hundred cubic feet of air a minute; they are meant for larger rooms.

How Air Cleaners Operate

Smoke particles, microbes, and many other solid contaminants are far smaller than the hair and dust you see floating in the air, narrower than the 10-micron threshold of visibility (a micron is about one twenty-five-thousandth of an inch). The gas molecules from smoke are many times smaller still. To remove such small particles, air cleaners typically use filters, electrical attraction, or ozone. Here are the basics of how the principal types work.

Filters. The finer a filter's sieve, the smaller the particles it traps. "High-efficiency particulate arresting" filters (HEPA, for short) snare at least 99.97 percent of particles larger than 0.3 micron. These filters were originally developed to trap radioactive dust in atomic plants. A variant, the pleated filter, traps at least 95 percent of the same particles. By comparison, a room air conditioner's foam filter traps particles only 10 microns or larger, and no more than 30 percent of them at that. But even the best HEPA filter can't catch something as small as a gas molecule. Activated carbon or charcoal filters, found on many HEPA- or pleated-filter air cleaners, are needed for that task.

Electrical attraction. There are three main types. In an electrostatic precipitating cleaner, a high-voltage wire charges particles drawn in by a fan, which are then attracted to a precipitating cell carrying the opposite electrical charge. An "electret" filter uses fibers with a static charge to trap particles. A negative-ion generator uses fine, electrically charged needles or wires to ionize particles, which collect in a filter or, more typically, on your walls and furnishings. None of the electrical-attraction cleaners remove gas molecules, which tend to diffuse back into the air.

Ozonation. An ozone generator uses a high-voltage electric charge to convert oxygen in the air to ozone, a pungent, powerful oxidant. At sufficiently high concentrations, ozone attacks and destroys gas molecules and microorganisms. Ozone has no effect on dust and other particulates, however. And ozone generators sold for home use can actually foul the air.

There is no universally accepted performance standard for comparing air cleaners. The closest thing to one is the clean air delivery rate (CADR), which expresses the number of cubic feet of clean air a unit delivers each minute. The CADR, developed and certified by the Association of Home Appliance Manufacturers, is used by some air-cleaner manufacturers on their products.

For rooms of various sizes, the CADR is based on both the percentage of particles removed and how quickly they are removed. Tests performed to the appliance association's specifications provide CADR numbers for dust, smoke, and pollen.

Consumers Union believes that CADR numbers alone don't provide a complete picture of an air cleaner's effectiveness. It's also necessary to know the unit's total air-flow rate to properly assess efficiency. Two cleaners may have the same CADR, but the one with the lower total air flow will be the more efficient.

Air flow. Room units move more air than tabletop models do. In Consumers Union's tests, air flows were 10 percent lower than what manufacturers claimed.

Odors. A telltale odor will linger long after you clear a room of tobacco smoke. That's because most air cleaners won't capture gases from the smoke, which stick to walls, furniture, and clothing, and which seep back into the air over time. Even the best air cleaners remove smoke particles far more effectively than they do smoke odors. It would take cleaners at least 10 times longer to remove odors than to remove smoke particles.

Noise. Few models are objectionably loud at their lowest fan speed, but many can be annoying at their highest speed. The lowest setting is generally preferable for continuous use. Because an air cleaner is often used in a bedroom at night, it is a good idea to listen to the machine you are planning to buy. If you can't try it in a quiet location in the store, be sure the air cleaner is returnable if it turns out to be too noisy at home.

MAINTENANCE AND OPERATING COSTS

A few air cleaners consume a minimal amount of electricity over the course of a year—less than $20 at the national average electric rate. Energy costs range more typically from about $20 to $40.

The cost of replacement filters can be quite high, however, particularly for units using a HEPA filter. Based on the manufacturers' recommended filter replacement intervals, HEPA filters may cost $50 to $140; other types of filters, $20 to $80 a year.

Most air cleaners require little maintenance beyond filter changes and cleanings. If you choose an electrostatic precipitator, you'll need to wash its electronic cell every few months.

RECOMMENDATIONS

Do what you can to minimize or eliminate sources of air pollution. You may be able to improve the air quality inside your house without spending hundreds of dollars on an air cleaner. Just opening a few windows may do the job. Even in winter, cracking open a window a couple of inches won't raise your heating bill by more than a few pennies an hour. In addition, a kitchen exhaust fan should effectively dispose of smoke and fumes from cooking.

But if you can't open a window—because the outside air is polluted or the temperature outside is bitter cold—or if you need to ventilate a windowless space, an air cleaner may be the only way to reduce smoke and airborne dust.

DEALING WITH ALLERGY

Simply setting up an air cleaner in the middle of the room will not reduce or prevent asthmatic attacks or offer relief from allergic and respiratory problems, according to Harold S. Nelson, M.D., of the National Jewish Center in Denver, who chaired a committee organized by the American Academy of Allergy and Immunology to study allergens in indoor air and air-cleaning devices.

"Most household dust is inert," he told Consumers Union. "Removing it from the air with [an air cleaner] won't help much. As for pollen, an air conditioner may be sufficient."

Dr. Nelson blames the fecal pellets of house dust mites (microscopic creatures that feed on human skin cells that have been sloughed off) for many allergic reactions. The pellets are too large to remain airborne for long; they settle within minutes, so an air cleaner is rather ineffective against them.

The problem is that the mites thrive in mattresses, pillows, and blankets. An allergy sufferer buries his or her face in the bedding, breathes in the pellets, and suffers an allergic reaction. The best relief comes from separating the patient from the allergen. The pillows and mattress should be sealed in special allergen-proof casings, available from surgical supply houses. Blankets and sheets should be washed often. For the same reason, allergy sufferers should avoid lying on an upholstered couch.

Some manufacturers promote humidifiers as beneficial for allergies. Dr. Nelson believes a humidifier can do more harm than good because house dust mites proliferate in humid conditions. He advises keeping indoor humidity relatively low, at about 20 to 30 percent. If you use a humidifier, clean it frequently and in accordance with the manufacturer's instructions.

Animal dander is lighter than most dust and tends to remain airborne longer, creating a serious problem for allergy sufferers. If you have a pet, at least keep the bedroom off limits. Here, an air cleaner might help, since the airborne particles of animal dander can be collected by these machines.

OZONE GENERATORS

Ozone can purify drinking water, disinfect mildewed boats, and deodorize fire-ravaged buildings. But ozone is also a toxic gas, a component of smog, with no known beneficial health effects.

The U.S. Occupational Safety and Health Administration limits ozone exposure in industrial settings to 100 parts per billion (ppb) over an eight-hour day, six days per week. At that level, ozone irritates the eyes, makes the throat feel dry, and stresses the lungs. The U.S. Food and Drug Administration has set a limit of 50 ppb for the ozone from electronic air cleaners. That's a sensible limit for the home.

Given those facts, an ozone-generating air cleaner would seem a contradiction in terms. To date, Consumers Union has not found a unit that allows users to measure ozone output or to control ozone levels in a meaningful way. Some promotional materials say you can tell if ozone levels are too high when the distinctive odor becomes apparent. But research has shown that odor isn't a reliable yardstick.

When Consumers Union tested ozone generators under a variety of conditions, they almost always produced ozone levels well above the FDA's limit of 50 ppb. Although ozone generators have limited value in unoccupied spaces, it's highly questionable whether they belong where people breathe.

WHOLE-HOUSE AIR CLEANERS

There are air cleaners designed to fit the ductwork for central heating or air-conditioning. The simplest type is a filter that replaces the system's existing one. It should be possible for you to install and replace them yourself.

More complex—and more expensive—are electrostatic precipitators, which should be installed by a contractor. You can buy these filters through heating and air-conditioning dealers, or at home centers. It can cost as much as $300 to have a professional install one of the electrostatic precipitators.

In tests that mimicked air flow through air ducts, in-duct electrostatic precipitators removed dust and smoke particles within a room about as effectively as the better room-sized portable cleaners. A disposable electret filter was only a notch less effective. A self-charging electrostatic filter was in the same league as a small tabletop air cleaner.

Any of these in-duct air cleaners may affect the overall performance of the heating and cooling system. The precipitators have no fan of their own, relying on the furnace or air conditioner to move air through the system. So when the thermostat shuts the system down, it will also shut down the air cleaner unless the system has a switch to keep the fan going continuously. In addition, the filters will slow air flow through the ducts. That may make the system run longer to heat or cool, increasing your energy bill.

If you have air-quality problems throughout the house that can't be controlled in any other way—and if ductwork is already in place—then the electrostatic precipitators could be useful. But if you just need to clean the air in a couple of rooms, a portable air cleaner would be a better choice.

AUTO POLISHES

One of the attractions of a new car is its showroom shine. Many newer models have an additional clear coating designed to add even more luster and durability to the finish. But eventually sunlight, water, air pollution, and other contaminants can age and erode the paint until the gloss fades, and the finish is no longer able to shed contaminants (e.g., water, dirt, etc.). At this point, auto polish can make a dramatic improvement.

You'll find auto polish in liquid, paste, and a few spray versions. The products are interchangeably labeled wax, polish, or sealant by their makers. The one-step applications contain abrasives or solvents to remove stubborn stains or oxidation from a car's finish and waxes or silicones that can fill tiny cracks and renew the water repellency of the finish.

EFFECTIVENESS

On car surfaces that are weathered, some polishes will shine better than others. Yet even the better ones won't increase the gloss of a new car. Some can make new paint look worse by leaving slight scratches or haze.

A major part of the sales appeal of auto polishes is the protection they're supposed to provide against the elements. But a polish can't protect anything once it has worn away. People who polish their cars may not do it often enough with most polishes.

If you want to see whether a polish is holding up, look at what happens to water on the car's surface. The beads of water that form on a protected surface are relatively small and rounded, and sit high on the surface. As the polish wears away, the beads spread and flatten. Eventually, when the polish is completely gone, water doesn't bead at all; it lies in a sheet on the surface.

Liquids are somewhat easier to apply and spread better than pastes, but all products should go on easily. Spray-on products are especially easy to apply. But be careful not to get the spray—or any polish, for that matter—on vinyl surfaces or on the windshield. The polish may affect the appearance of the vinyl. (Be sure to shake a liquid or spray container before you begin; some of the ingredients may have settled to the bottom.)

Instructions on the labels of most nonspray polishes call for spreading them on with an applicator (which is provided with some products), letting them dry to a haze, and buffing with a dry, soft cotton cloth. Buffing is likely to be fairly easy with most. But a few products dry into a rather stiff coating that needs more effort to buff. You should never polish a car in direct sunlight when the surface is hot to the touch. The paint can soften and be susceptible to scratching.

ABRASIVENESS

The paint, not the polish, protects a car's metal from rust. So it makes sense to polish away no more paint than is necessary to restore a smooth finish. If you're using a polish for the first time on your car, test it on an inconspicuous part of the car. It should remove any oxidation or contaminants but shouldn't leave a haze or scratches. On older cars that do not have a clear top coat, polish should not remove much of the color.

A fine abrasive is useful for removing stubborn stains or oxidation. For an extremely weathered finish, however, even the most abrasive polishes may not be adequate. Special, highly abrasive polishing or rubbing compounds are available for such challenging jobs. They are usually found right next to the auto polishes in the store. But do not rub too long or too hard with them, or you may rub right through the paint to the primer.

RECOMMENDATIONS

Whichever polish you use, be sure to wash the car thoroughly beforehand. Most road dirt is a good deal harder than a car's finish. If you polish a dirty car, you'll only grind the dirt into the paint, scratching the finish as you rub.

You may not need to polish a new car, but you should wash it often. Bird and tree droppings, salt, tar, and even plain dirt can eventually mar the finish. Frequent washing is especially important in the summer, when high temperatures increase the damaging effects of contaminants.

Paint Removal

When you have to deal with paint that's in really poor condition, you may have to go beyond just stripping away the flaking and peeling paint. If you don't, the surface—whether that of furniture, walls, or the side of a house—may continue to deteriorate. You'd probably have far better results if you stripped off *all* the old paint.

Before you remove any paint, find out if it contains any lead. Lead paint—or more precisely, lead-containing dust from leaded paint in the home—is a major cause of childhood lead poisoning. Many children have accidentally been poisoned when the process of remodeling in an older home spread lead dust. If your home or apartment building was built more than 20 years ago, it may contain leaded paint. If it is more than 50 years old, it is almost certain that there is some lead paint. Intact lead paint, covered with layers of unleaded paint, is essentially harmless. But improper removal that turns the lead loose can create a severe hazard.

If you do have lead paint to remove, dust control is critical. You should, therefore, choose a chemical stripper. If you are sure the paint you need to strip is lead-free, choose any of the three basic methods—chemical, mechanical, or heat—based on each method's pros and cons. Most do-it-yourselfers use chemicals and/or heat guns for all kinds of interior woodwork: furniture, doors, moldings, and the like.

Chemical strippers soften and dislodge the old finish so you can scrape it off. They are sold as liquids, gels, or pastes; some are more toxic than others.

Heat is delivered via heat guns. Some people use a propane torch, but the open flame can char wood or even start a fire. By blowing air that can reach temperatures greater than 800°F, these devices—which resemble a blow-dryer—cause paint to blister and bubble; then you scrape.

Mechanical stripping relies on such tools as scrapers and sandpaper, power sanders, and gadgets that attach to drills. Because they can scratch, these tools shouldn't be used on smooth or delicate surfaces.

Rather than try to strip the paint yourself, you can farm out the work to professionals. A pro is likely to do a more thorough job, and the price is usually reasonable.

TESTING FOR LEAD PAINT

Consider hiring a trained person to do a lead hazard assessment. This involves testing representative paint surfaces with a portable X-ray fluorescence device that produces instant results and can even find lead paint buried under layers of unleaded paint. It also includes taking samples of dirt from the floors and window sills to be analyzed in a laboratory. An assessment should cost about $300 for an average-size house.

Another way to tell whether your home has lead paint is to use one of the do-it-yourself or mail-in kits available for that purpose. With the do-it-yourself kits, you cut, scrape, or sand a small patch to expose layers of paint. Then you use a chemical reagent—either rhodizonate or sodium sulfide—that changes color if the paint contains lead. With rhodizonate kits, the warning color—pink—is easy to see unless the paint itself is red or pink. Sodium sulfide kits indicate lead with a gray to black color, so it is hard to see a positive reaction on dark paint. These kits clearly indicate high levels of lead, but some may not detect levels slightly above the 0.06 percent legal limit in paint. Although this percentage is much lower than the levels in most old paint, the levels these kits can miss are still too high for safety, especially for households with children. Two kits—*Acc-U-Test* ($7) and *The Lead Detective* ($30)—were found to be sensitive down to 0.05 percent. They're good on light-colored paints.

Mail-in kits (costing about $20) can detect lead levels down to 0.05 percent. They include a plastic bag, plastic gloves, and a form to fill out and return with the paint sample. The cost includes analysis of one sample by a government-certified lab. Results are likely to be much more accurate than those obtained from home kits. Mail-in kits also say *how much* lead is present, not just whether it is there or not. Consumers Union found the *Clean Water Lead in Paint Kit* to provide a rapid—about 2 weeks—turnaround.

CHEMICAL PAINT REMOVERS

If you have lead paint to remove, choose a chemical stripper. Some chemical paint removers are made with volatile solvents—methanol (wood alcohol), toluene, and acetone. Although they're cheaper and faster than some less toxic types, they leave a waxy film that you may need to remove with mineral spirits. But this is the least of their problems. Most are highly flammable, and their vapors can cause headaches and, after continued and prolonged exposure, nerve damage.

In the world of solvent strippers, those made with methylene chloride stand alone. A mainstay of paint-removal products for years, methylene chloride can soften and dislodge a variety of tough finishes, including polyurethanes and epoxies, and isn't flammable. But exposure to its fumes can lead to kidney disease, an irregular heartbeat, even heart attack. The solvent is considered a possible human carcinogen, based on persuasive animal studies.

Any solvent-based paint remover, whether it uses volatile solvents or methylene chloride, can be dangerous to use indoors, even with a window open. Protective garb is essential—neoprene gloves (dishwashing gloves will dissolve), goggles, and a respirator to keep you from inhaling fumes.

LESS HAZARDOUS CHEMICALS

The past few years have seen the introduction of chemical strippers that pose fewer risks than the solvent products. Almost odor-free as well as safer to breathe, they are less likely to irritate skin. Cleanup is easier, too. Once the softened paint has been scraped, light scrubbing with a wet sponge or rag will clear away any remaining residue.

The safer products, however, are very slow to show results. A solvent stripper might remove several coats of paint in two or three hours. A nonsolvent stripper would have to sit from six hours to overnight. To make matters worse, some nonsolvent varieties dry out, which means you have to brush additional remover over the slightly moist paint. Look for products that come with plastic-coated paper that's applied over the substance to keep it moist.

HEAT GUNS

If you know you have lead paint to strip, never use a heat gun. They can increase your exposure to lead by whipping paint dust into the air, where you can inhale it. When the dust settles, it can still be hazardous to young children.

Using a heat gun is intense work, but it's faster than any chemical method. Unlike chemicals, heat guns rarely have to go over the same area twice. Once the hot paint separates from the underlying surface, you can peel it off easily.

After the initial expense, heat guns are cheap to use. But they do have limitations. They're frustrating to use when the paint film is very thin (they work best when bubbling up several layers); they won't remove varnish or other clear coatings; and they're ineffective on painted metal. (Metal conducts heat too rapidly.)

Heat guns also have hazards. The expelled-air temperature may be as high as 875ºF—high enough to cause a severe burn or even start a fire. Also, it's easy to ignore where you're pointing the gun as you dig out a persistent bit of paint. Always keep a wet rag and a bucket of water handy.

Even if you're never blasted by the gun's hot air, you can get burned by touching the metal nozzle. This is a serious concern, especially if you put down the gun near a child or curious pet. It is essential to look for models that have a fan that runs at a Low or Cold setting to hasten cooling.

Professional Stripping

Professional paint removers have one big advantage over do-it-yourselfers: they use a tank. By immersing items that need paint removed in a cavernous vat of potent chemicals, professionals can get the last traces of paint out of nooks and crannies.

"Dip" stripping systems differ significantly. Some rely on corrosive lye; others on solvents. When you contact a professional paint remover, it's a good idea to ask which method of paint removal will be used.

A remover who uses lye will dunk the painted object in a lye and water solution. The softened paint is scraped off, and the item is neutralized and rinsed with water. It's an inexpensive and effective treatment—too effective, in fact. Lye not only dissolves paint; it can also stain wood fibers, raise their grain (making wood feel "fuzzy"), and extract natural resins. In addition, immersion can dissolve glues and swell wood so badly that it warps or falls apart. This won't happen if the operator removes the item from the tank as soon as the paint is softened. In practice, however, such care is not always exercised.

Professional paint removers, whose workplaces are regulated by the Occupational Safety and Health Administration, achieve better results with the solvent method. Oversoaking is less likely to produce ruined goods. Still, because some companies that use solvents on items rinse them in water, wood grain can rise and iron parts can rust. Fortunately, there are solvent systems that avoid the use of water.

Consumers Union testers took old chairs and shutters to two professional paint removers. Both stripped with solvents: one used methylene chloride, hand scraping, and a water washdown; the other used xylol and dimethyl formamide (DMF), first as a bath and then in a spray that dislodged the softened paint. DMF worked very well. The methylene chloride cleaning was a bit less satisfactory: The shutter had some raised grain and mild rust on its fittings; the chair retained patches of paint and showed signs of too much scraping.

RECOMMENDATIONS

First, make sure you don't have lead paint. If you do, choose a chemical stripper. Do not use a heat gun.

Any chemical or heat gun will remove paint, which makes the

safety factor paramount. Solvent-based strippers, particularly those containing methylene chloride, pose serious health hazards when used indoors. Adequate ventilation may not be enough. Protect your eyes and hands, and wear a respirator. If you choose a solvent product, try to use it outdoors. Better yet, consider going to a professional paint remover, who is likely to do a better job. But this won't work for built-in cabinets, window frames, baseboards, and other nonremovable woodwork.

For immovable items, such as banisters, moldings, and door jambs, try a heat gun (if lead is not a factor) or one of the less toxic chemicals. Although the nonsolvent products are slow and expensive, they're safer than the others.

Heat guns work faster than chemicals but require precautions to minimize charring and the risk of burns and fire. However, heat guns aren't effective on metal and won't strip clear finishes. Don't succumb to the seemingly attractive idea of mounting a scraping blade on the nozzle of a heat gun. It doesn't take long for the softened paint to pile up. When it does, you have to remove it. Steer clear of any device that encourages probing around the tip of a hot heat gun.

MECHANICAL PAINT REMOVERS

Scrapers, rasps, and sandpaper substitutes are available. Each type has its uses, however specialized. Since none is really expensive, it's a good idea to keep more than one type in your tool kit. For chemical or solvent stripping of fine furniture, use wood or plastic scrapers to avoid gouging the surface. Because they create lots of chips and dust, these methods should not be used to remove lead paint.

Hook scrapers. A hook scraper is best suited for removing loose paint from flat surfaces. It looks something like an extra-large razor with a stiff, fairly dull blade. And like a razor, it's pulled along the work surface, so the edge of the blade scrapes away the paint.

Push scrapers. These resemble the familiar putty knife, although they vary in details. Some have a long handle, others a short one. Some have a blunt edge, others are sharpened. You have your choice of stiff or flexible blades in several widths; the differences are of minor importance. You should try to match the shape and size of the scraper to the job at hand—a narrow-bladed scraper, for example, will work best in and around window frames. Push scrapers are useful on flat surfaces and for digging paint out of corners, but they are not meant to be used on curves. In general, they are less effective than hook scrapers on all but the loosest paint. It's harder to push a scraper than to pull it.

Rasps and abrasive blocks. These devices can scrape and sand, and are generally available in a variety of sizes and abrasive grades. Rasps and blocks can also be used for sanding wood. Their shape, however, limits their use primarily to flat surfaces.

Sandpaper substitutes. Unlike rasps and sanding blocks, sandpaper substitutes are fairly flexible, so they can get into places that the others can't. Typically, they are rectangles of tough cloth coated on both sides with sheets of abrasive-coated nylon mesh, or a thin sheet of metal punched with ragged holes. Sandpaper substitutes are durable and fast cutting; they can be wrapped around a dowel to sand a concave surface or can be used with a sanding block. Some may leave the surface rather rough, making it necessary to do some sanding before painting.

Sponges and glass blocks. To sand moldings and other complex shapes, woodworkers often wrap sandpaper around a sponge. Sanding sponges come essentially prewrapped, with an abrasive coating that covers four sides. They are springy and flexible, as you'd expect sponges to be. They can also be rinsed out to un-clog the abrasive. Foamed glass blocks resemble chunks of hard-ened plastic foam. They wear away quite rapidly as they're used, leaving a residue of glass dust in the work area.

Steel wool. Do not use steel wool where the fine metal shards may be exposed to water (including water-based varnishes) be-cause steel wool rusts and leaves a visible stain.

SAFETY

Paint removal, especially with power tools, requires certain safety precautions. To guard against the obvious hazard—flying chips of paint or grit—you should wear safety goggles or a face shield, work gloves, and a heavy jacket. Hearing protectors are also ad-visable.

You should guard against health hazards that may not be im-mediately apparent, such as the problem of lead. The key to preparing lead-painted surfaces for repainting is dust control. If you're doing the job yourself, take the following precautions:

- Thoroughly cover the area with heavy plastic drop cloths.
- Remove furniture or wrap it in plastic.
- Tape plastic over doors and windows.
- Wear plastic booties over your shoes.
- Rent or buy a HEPA respirator designed to filter lead dust. Keep it on while disposing of the drop cloths and plastic coverings.
- Wet the surface with a spray bottle before scraping or sanding with a wet/dry abrasive.
- Instead of sanding to "rough up" a glossy surface, use a chem-ical etcher.
- Thoroughly clean all surfaces after the stripping process. Scrub with water plus a phosphate detergent. If you live in an area that bans phosphate, try using a powdered dishwasher detergent.

■ Wring out the sponge, mop, or rag in a separate bucket so you don't recycle the lead in the cleaning solution, and change the rinse water frequently.

If you hire a contractor, be sure to find one who will use these techniques. Look for a contractor who is certified or licensed for lead safety. Otherwise, you could prepare the most deteriorated spots to paint yourself, then hire a regular contractor to do the rest—with strict instructions not to sand or scrape.

POWER BLOWERS

People use a power blower to clean up leaves and spread grass clippings after mowing, to vacuum debris from decks and side-walks, even to dry up puddles in the driveway. These versatile machines take some of the work out of tidying a lawn. But with more blowers running longer for more of the year, the noise from a blower—about the same as that from a very loud lawn mower—has become an unacceptable intrusion in hundreds of communities. More than 280 towns and cities have restricted the use of power blowers, and a handful have banned them entirely.

Noise level is one of the factors when looking at gasoline-powered and electric handheld blowers (the kind most people buy), as well as backpack models similar to those used by the pros. Most of the handheld blowers work as both a vacuum and as a blower; some lower-priced models are blowers only.

Electric blowers, the quieter type, used to be considerably weaker than gasoline-powered ones. But fairly quiet gas blowers and powerful electrics both exist.

HOW THEY PERFORM

Noise. Gasoline-powered models produce enough noise to warrant wearing ear protectors. The average electric blower typically creates about half the racket of a gasoline model and so doesn't demand hearing protection. The noisiest gas-powered blowers might make you less popular with the neighbors.

Blowing power. A blower's effectiveness at piling up leaves is not necessarily related to engine size and horsepower or motor amperage, or to the manufacturer's claimed nozzle air speed.

The best way to assess a blower's effectiveness is to blow leaves into elongated rows. The most powerful blowers can build rows 18 inches high—the weakest, only 8 to 10 inches. That may not seem like much of a range, but a pile 18 inches high may contain more than three times as many leaves as one 10 inches high. The weakest power blowers are adequate only if you

BACKPACK BLOWERS

Professional lawn-care services use backpack blowers. The backpack's weight, in the neighborhood of 20 pounds, isn't a drawback once the unit is donned and properly adjusted. It's also much less fatiguing than a hand-held blower for big lawn-cleaning jobs. For the most part, backpack blowers are comfortable and easy to handle, and several have conveniences like a handle with the throttle and On/Off switches on the blower tube, a large fuel-filler opening, and a throttle control you can preset.

Nevertheless, these high-priced machines have limitations. They don't vacuum. They are all very loud. And, despite their size, they aren't inherently more powerful than regular blowers. In fact, several handheld models can equal the blowing power of the best backpacks. Unless you have a big yard or a yen to look like a pro, there's little reason to buy a backpack.

have a small lawn, or if you mainly need to clear driveways and other hard surfaces.

Blower cleaning. A blower may have the power to pile up plenty of leaves but still lack some lawn-cleaning ability. You should assess a blower's ability to rid a lawn of all leaves in areas with heavy leaf accumulations amid grass about three inches high.

The blowers that clean best are those with a round-end blower nozzle. All the so-so blowers have a "diffuser" nozzle that's roughly rectangular at the end.

Blower handling. A blower handles well if it's easy to move in a sweeping side-to-side motion. A good blower should also be easy to hold in the odd and varying positions sometimes necessary for cleaning out tight spots.

Two forces conspire to make handling more difficult: the downward thrust caused by the curved shape of most blower nozzles, and the resistance to back-and-forth motion generated by models with a horizontal driveshaft.

One feature helped mitigate the effect of the downward thrust: a comfortable, well-positioned second handle.

HOW THEY VACUUM

Speed. The collection bags that come with blowers don't hold enough to make them practical for vacuuming an entire lawn, even though the machines shred vacuumed material to greatly reduce its volume. But these machines are handy for vacuuming leaves away from shrubs, flower beds, and other places where raking or blowing proves impractical.

Handling. The easiest blowers to handle have effective, well-positioned, and comfortable handles; don't vibrate much; and don't make you stoop to hold the end of the suction tube at ground level.

CONVENIENCE

Blowers judged convenient typically had these handy features: For gasoline-powered models, a starter cord near the engine housing's center line, so pulling the cord didn't make the blower twist; an engine-kill switch you can reach with the same hand that holds the main handle; and a throttle that lets you preset two or more positions. For electric blowers, an On/Off switch that you can reach with the hand holding the main handle and a second, lower-speed setting for those times when you don't need too much power.

WATER TREATMENT

Public concern over the quality of drinking water often centers on how the water looks, smells, or tastes. But such aesthetic problems are usually caused by calcium, sulfur, chlorine, or iron, which are harmless. Of more concern are pollutants such as lead, radon, and nitrate, which pose a health hazard.

Before buying any equipment or taking the expensive route of buying bottled water, find out what's in your water.

You can ask the water company for a copy of its latest water analysis. Or, if you draw water from a private well, call the local public health department to find out about any groundwater problems. (If testing is warranted, see page 134.)

Water-treatment devices range from simple filtering carafes and faucet attachments to whole-house systems. They're sold in places as diverse as drugstores and TV home-shopping networks. As a rule, hardware stores, home centers, department stores, and mass merchandisers sell the more modest devices for as little as $20. Sophisticated systems, which can cost more than $1000, are sold by water treatment dealers and direct-marketing companies. Major brands include Ametek, Amway, Brita, Culligan, Glacier Pure,

Instapure (Teledyne/WaterPik), Mr. Coffee, NSA, Omni, Pollenex, Rainsoft, and Sears.

PROBLEM POLLUTANTS

Lead. Chronic lead exposure, even at low levels, could cause permanent learning disabilities and hyperactivity. It's particularly dangerous for pregnant women and children. In adults, chronic exposure is linked to high blood pressure and anemia.

Lead gets into water primarily through corrosion of household plumbing and the service line (the pipe connecting the home plumbing with the water main). Installation of lead service lines has been banned for nearly a decade, but many homes more than 30 years old still have them. They may also have copper pipes with lead solder (also banned). Lead in water can also come from brass in faucets and well pumps.

Since 1991, the U.S. Environmental Protection Agency (EPA) has required water companies to run spot tests for lead contamination. If more than 10 percent of the households checked have lead levels above 15 parts per billion (ppb), the company will have to take action, either by treating the water or by replacing lead service lines. The deadline for companies serving more than 50,000 people is January 1997; smaller systems have until 1999.

In 1992, *Consumer Reports* tested water in the homes of 2,643 readers in eight cities, finding worrisome results in some cities, including Chicago, New York, and Boston. Later, 1,280 homes in those cities and in Portland and St. Paul, where the EPA had found fairly high lead levels, were tested.

The water supply in Chicago had improved considerably. New York showed modest improvement. Although Boston has been treating the water in its reservoir for years, results still show room for improvement. Lead concentrations remained too high in St. Paul even after running the water. In Portland, first-draw water (which has stood in the pipes for hours) had moderate levels of lead; purged-line water (drawn after running for a while) had almost no lead.

To minimize your exposure to lead from pipes, use only cold water for cooking and drinking; hot water dissolves more lead. Running the water for a minute or so to flush the pipes may help, but it's not a sure cure. If you have more than 5 ppb of lead in your water even after letting it run, you need to take action.

Radon. This probably poses a greater health risk than any other waterborne pollutant. According to the EPA, radon, a naturally occurring radioactive gas, may cause more than 10,000 lung-cancer deaths each year. Most of the radon seeps into homes from the ground. But some well water contains dissolved radon, which escapes into the air from showers and washers.

Waterborne radon is usually confined to private wells or small community water systems that use wells. Before testing water for radon, test the air inside your house for radon. If the level is high

---

WHERE TO GET YOUR WATER TESTED

Companies that sell water-treatment equipment often offer a free or low-cost water analysis. Don't depend on that kind of test: The results may be biased. Instead, ask your water company, health department, or cooperative extension agency for a referral. You can also check the Yellow Pages under "Laboratories—Testing," or contact a mail-order laboratory.

To get water tested for lead by mail, contact any of the following: Clean Water Lead Test Inc., Asheville, N.C., 704 251-6800 ($17); Environmental Law Foundation, Oakland, Calif., 510 208-4555 ($16.50); SAVE, New York, N.Y., 718 626-3936 ($20).

Avoid do-it-yourself home testing kits.

---

and you use well water, have the water tested. If the level of radon in the air is low, don't worry about the water.

Although experts disagree as to the level of radon you should do something about, you should take action if the level in the water is 10,000 picocuries per liter or higher. Radon is easily dispersed in outdoor air, so aerating the water before it enters the house is usually the simplest solution. Ventilating the bathroom, laundry room, or kitchen may also help.

Nitrate. High nitrate levels in water pose a risk mainly to infants. Bacteria in immature digestive tracts convert nitrate into nitrite; that combines with hemoglobin in the blood to form methemoglobin, which cannot transport oxygen. The resulting ailment, methemoglobinemia, is rare but can result in brain damage or death. Some adults, including pregnant women, may also be susceptible.

Chemical fertilizers and animal wastes are prime sources of nitrate contamination, so homes in agricultural areas with private wells should have their water tested regularly. Some state health departments test wells for free. High nitrate levels may also signal the presence of other contaminants.

TREATMENT METHODS

The chart on pages 136–37 shows which technologies work best for which substances. Some products, called single-stage filters, use one of the methods explained below; others, called multistage filters, combine two or more. *Note:* None are suitable for treating bacteriologically contaminated water, which requires sterilization with ultraviolet rays, ozone, or chlorine.

Carbon filtration. This is the most popular method of water treatment. Carbon filters overcome a variety of problems. They remove residual chlorine, improving the water's taste. They can also remove organic compounds such as pesticides, solvents, and chlo-

WATER PROBLEMS AND SOLUTIONS

Action is recommended if your drinking water contains more

	Maximum contaminant level [1]	Carbon filter
Aesthetic problems		
Dissolved iron	—	
Rust stains	—	
Calcium	—	
Magnesium	—	
Chlorine	—	✔
Salty taste	—	
"Skunky" taste	—	✔
Total dissolved solids	500 ppm	
Health hazards—organic		
Benzine	5 ppb	✔
Carbon tetrachloride	5 ppb	✔
Lindane	0.2 ppb	✔
Methoxychlor	40 ppb	✔
Trichloroethylene	5 ppb	✔
Trihalomethanes (THM)	100 ppb	✔
Health hazards—inorganic		
Arsenic	50 ppb	
Barium	2 ppm	
Cadmium	5 ppb	
Chromium	100 ppb	
Fluoride	2.2 ppm	
Lead	15 ppb [3]	[4]
Mercury	2 ppb	✔
Nitrate	10 ppm	
Selenium	10 ppb	
Health hazards—radiological		
Dissolved radon	10,000 pc/l	✔

[1] *ppm = parts per million; ppb = parts per billion; pc/l = piccocuries per liter.*   [2] *Most will*

than the maximum contaminant level.

Reverse osmosis [2]	Distiller	Water softener	Activated alumina cartridge	Aerator
		✔		
	✔			
		✔		
		✔		
	✔			✔
✔	✔			
✔	✔			
				✔
				✔
	✔			
	✔			
				✔
✔	✔			
✔	✔	✔		
✔	✔	✔		
✔	✔			
✔	✔		✔	
✔	✔		✔	
✔	✔			
✔	✔			
✔	✔		✔	
				✔

also remove organic substances.   [3] Action level.   [4] Some will remove lead.

roform. Some carbon filters are effective for lead; some aren't. The whole-house variety is especially useful for removing radon.

Where lead contamination is known to be a problem, a larger filter is better. Small pour-through filters and fist-sized units that thread onto the faucet can improve the taste of water, but they're only moderately effective against hazardous chemicals. There, a high-volume undersink or countertop filter is the best choice. Replaceable filter cartridges made either with a "carbon block" or granulated carbon are better than those made with powdered carbon.

Reverse osmosis (RO). This method excels at removing inorganic contaminants, such as dissolved salts, ferrous iron, chloride, fluoride, nitrate, and heavy metals such as lead. RO works slowly, producing only a few gallons of fresh water per day, and is wasteful—for every gallon of water purified, several gallons are wasted.

Most RO systems use a carbon filter. They have a second filter, a cellophanelike semipermeable membrane that's easily clogged by minerals in hard water. (To extend its life, install a separate sediment prefilter upstream of the carbon filter. A 5- to 10-micron mesh is fine enough.) The membrane needs replacement every few years, carbon filters more often.

Distillation. Distillation improves the taste of brackish water, and it demineralizes water polluted with heavy metals. But it's ineffective against volatile organics like chloroform and benzene, which vaporize in the distiller and wind up in the condensed water. The process is slow—it takes a couple of hours to produce a quart of water—and uses a lot of electricity. Since it collects and concentrates minerals, scale can build up quickly and must be cleaned out.

Water softeners. Water softeners remove hard water minerals, stain-producing iron and, in some cases, lead. They don't remove radon, nitrate, or pesticides.

Systems vary in size, but all consist of a large tank near the main supply of water to a house. As a result, softeners are effective against lead only if contamination occurs in service lines outside the house.

Activated alumina. If lead is your only problem, activated alumina cartridges, which come in faucet-mounted filters and in-line units, are an effective treatment.

Aeration. Aerators are effective at removing chlorine, radon, benzene, carbon tetrachloride, and trihalomethanes.

TREATMENT PRODUCTS

Reverse-osmosis devices are installed in the water line under the sink by a professional. They have their own spigot and storage tank. If your household needs maximum lead removal, consider one of these. Their large storage tank holds a supply of treated water ample enough for most uses. Operation cost is fairly low. However, if you should empty the tank, you'll have to wait two or three hours for it to process another gallon.

Distillers, which aren't plumbed in, sit on the counter and are plugged into an electric outlet. They're a good choice if you need highly effective lead removal and don't consume a lot of water. Although cheaper to buy than a reverse-osmosis system, they're much more expensive to operate.

Undersink filters are plumbed in and have their own spigot. This type is best suited for a household that uses a lot of water. It produces purified water on demand, at a rate of about one-third gallon a minute. They're less expensive and easier to install than reverse-osmosis devices. An undersink filter can be installed by a do-it-yourselfer whose counter has an opening for the unit's spigot or who is willing to drill an opening.

Countertop filters sit next to the sink and attach to the existing faucet with flexible tubing. Like an undersink filter, a countertop model provides filtered water on demand, but it requires no major changes in plumbing. This type of unit takes up counter space, and its connector tubes can get in the way when you're using the sink.

A faucet-mounted filter is similar to a countertop unit, but it has no tubing at all, is smaller, and sits atop the faucet. It gives purified water on demand without taking up counter space or requiring much installation. But you may not like the way it looks perched on your faucet, and it may get in your way.

Carafe filters are stand-alone units that require no connection to the plumbing. They sit on a counter; you simply pour water through them. Water poured into the top compartment trickles through the filter and collects in the pitcher below. A carafe is best used to process only small amounts of water, perhaps a gallon or two a day.

RECOMMENDATIONS

The chart on pages 136–37 summarizes the best methods for the most common water problems. Before doing business with a water-treatment company you don't know, call the Better Business Bureau or a local consumer-protection agency to find out whether any complaints against the company are unresolved.

DRINKING WATER: IS IT SAFE TO SOFTEN THE RULES?

When you turn on the tap for a glass of water, you probably don't wonder whether it's safe to drink. You don't have to: It usually is. However, Congress may scale back the regulations that help keep your water that way as legislators consider changing the Safe Drinking Water Act.

The act, approved in 1974, was originally passed because some of the thousands of water systems in the United States were simply not delivering clean water.

The regulations have had a good effect. All public water systems that use surface water now must disinfect it, and most must filter it. And restrictions on lead in drinking water should help protect 600,000 children who might otherwise have unsafe amounts of lead in their blood.

But on occasion, people still get sick from contaminants in their water. The most readily recognized are acute outbreaks of illness caused by microbes. In the best-known such incident, in 1993, hundreds of thousands of Milwaukee residents were sickened and more than 100 killed by cryptosporidium, a microbe not yet covered by water regulations. It's harder to know how many people are harmed by chronic, low-level exposure to pathogens and chemical contaminants.

Setting limits. Under the Safe Drinking Water Act, the Environmental Protection Agency originally set monitoring requirements and contaminant limits for 26 substances that can taint drinking water. The debate over the effectiveness of the act dates back to 1986, when Congress directed the EPA—which had been lackadaisically implementing the act—to add 57 more substances, such as benzene and dioxin, to the list of contaminants that water systems must monitor and limit. Congress also told the EPA to add 25 new contaminants to the list every three years.

Those changes, critics say, cost too much. Nearly 90 percent of the nation's 58,000 community water systems are small ones, serving fewer than 3,300 people. Many of those systems say they have neither the staff nor the money to obey the 1986 regulations.

Indeed, in 1994, community water systems were cited for about 100,000 violations of the Safe Drinking Water Act. Most of those cited were small systems that were not complying with monitoring and reporting requirements rather than systems found to have dirty water.

Complying with the regulations could add several hundred dollars a year to the water bills paid by customers of some small water systems.

Realistic regulations. Under pressure from water companies, local officials, and governors, the Senate came up with a plan for lightening the burden on water suppliers.

Small systems' testing requirements would be eased. Already, a state can let a water system skip particular tests if its water source is protected from contamination, or if a particular contaminant, such as a pesticide, was never used in the area. Under the proposal, states could issue testing exemptions much more freely.

Also, for any contaminants that don't cause acute health problems, the water systems would be able to test just once a year, or in some cases once every three years if the first test was clean, instead of quarterly testing.

Rules for cleaning up contamination would be lighter too. The EPA would require cleanup technologies that the small systems could more realistically afford, rather than base its standards on the best available methods that a large system can afford.

What's more, the proposed law would allow water systems that serve as many as 10,000 people to fail to meet federal health standards, if they can't afford to comply and if no unreasonable health risk would be created. As of 1995, only the very smallest systems—those that serve fewer than 500 households—can obtain such a waiver.

Finally, the bill proposes that the federal government give the states a total of $1 billion in loans and grants to help small water systems improve their facilities.

Going too far. It makes sense for Congress to revise a law that doesn't adequately account for the limited staff and resources of small water systems. No one is being served if those suppliers are just racking up violations instead of actually testing their water. But just as the 1986 law is too broad, so are the proposed revisions.

The problem is that the Senate bill doesn't just give small water systems a break; it also eases up on the large systems that serve most Americans.

The standards for cleanup technology would be made more lenient for large systems—an unnecessary move. And the bill would grant water systems three to five years to comply with any new or revised federal health standards, up from 18 months.

The bill also gives the EPA five or six years to develop several new standards that are already behind schedule. The limit on arsenic in drinking water, which dates from 1942, was to have been revised in 1989. Now it won't be updated until 2001. Limits on "disinfection byproducts," such as the potentially cancer-causing compounds created when chlorine is added to water, once were due in 1989 but now could be delayed until 2000. Existing court orders requiring the EPA to issue rules for about a dozen contaminants would be nullified. Even the rules being developed to thwart cryptosporidium could be delayed by extra regulatory hurdles.

What's more, the pace of new contaminant limits could be greatly slowed. Instead of setting standards for 25 contaminants every three years, the EPA would have to consider just five by 2001.

Those changes are a false economy. It's unwise to act as though we know there are few new contaminants of any consequence to be found. For people served by large water systems, the water bill would go up only about $25 a year if all the EPA regulations go into effect on schedule. That seems like a small price to pay to be sure that the water is safe.

Personal Care

FACIAL CLEANSERS

The main purpose of a facial cleanser is to remove makeup and grime. Soap and water do that, of course, but too much soap can remove a skin's natural oils, leaving it rough, chapped, and tender. Soap and water also have less clout than cleanser in removing heavy makeup.

A typical cleanser, whether cream or lotion, contains water; glycerine or other moisturizers; oils, fats, or greases (to give the product the right consistency and to help loosen grime); detergents (to wash away grime); preservatives (to forestall spoilage); and dyes and scent (to make it look and smell good).

The archetypal cleanser is the traditional "cold cream" that you massage into your skin, then wipe off. *Pond's Cold Cream* and its descendants—including wipe-off lotions—are still very popular. Years ago, however, *Noxzema* cream in the blue jar pointed the way toward a revolutionary alternative: a less greasy substance you can wash off with water. Today, there are as many wash-off creams and lotions as there are those that you have to wipe off. There are also creams and lotions that you can remove either way. The results of use tests conducted by Consumers Union showed that the preferences for cleansers specified by their makers for normal, dry, oily, or "combination" skin seemed to have no connection with skin type. Some women with dry skin preferred oily-skin products, some with normal skin liked dry-skin formulations, and so on.

PREFERENCES

An effective cleanser should be easy to apply and remove, take off makeup efficiently, smell pleasant, feel good on the skin during use, and leave the skin feeling nice.

Some cleansers are hard to remove. Removing some of the wash-off products can take more than a dozen rinses.

Cleansers should leave the skin feeling nice ("smooth" or "creamy"), but some may leave the skin feeling slightly coated, or dry and stiff. And some may leave the skin feeling greasy.

Most products have a scent, ranging in type from medicinal through spicy to floral. Some cleansers claim to be fragrance-free, but most of those have their own smell from ingredients not added for their fragrance, which you may or may not find pleasing.

Scent can play an important if unconscious role in judgment of overall quality. When Consumers Union's panelists scored a product low in smell, they generally gave it a low overall score.

COST, SIZE, QUALITY

Cleansers come in a variety of sizes. The price range is astonishingly wide, as it often is in the world of cosmetics. Price per ounce can vary considerably with container size.

FACIAL TISSUES

Tissues are used to handle all sorts of jobs—to wipe eyeglasses, to remove makeup, and as a stand-in for a napkin or a towel. But you expect most from a tissue when your nose runs nonstop and your eyes water. A tissue shouldn't shred when you sneeze into it, and you don't want one so harsh and scratchy that it chafes your nose. Yet you want something fairly economical. If the tissues are packed in a box to match your decor, so much the better.

QUALITY

Consumers Union tested tissues for sneeze resistance, wet strength, and softness. Since people can't be expected to sneeze on demand or to sneeze exactly the same way time after time, Consumers Union invented a mechanical sneezer to test tissues. The most sneeze-resistant tissues usually withstood the test just fine, but the worst were almost always shot through.

To measure strength when wet, testers clamped each tissue in an embroidery hoop, dampened it with a measured amount of water, then poured a slow, steady stream of lead shot onto the tissue. The strongest ones held more than 10 ounces of shot before they broke; they are the tissues you can count on to handle the most demanding jobs without disintegrating. The weakest tissues ruptured under about one ounce of weight. The thickest tissues tested were the three-ply, which weren't the strongest. Several two-ply varieties were even stronger; some others were just as strong.

Manufacturers often make facial tissues in more than one plant around the country to cut down on shipping costs. This practice could create variations in the same brand of tissue purchased in different areas. With few exceptions, however, the tissues bought from stores in the East, South, and West were quite consistent.

RECOMMENDATIONS

It doesn't make much sense to spend a lot of money on a throwaway product like facial tissue. But it does make sense to buy tissues that are reasonably soft, suitably strong, and low in price. The softest tissues are obviously the most soothing for a prolonged cold or bout of hay fever. Those with only average softness are fine for everyday use.

Hand Soaps

Soaps were the first surface-active agents prepared by man. They are the salts of water-insoluble fatty acids. Detergents are chemically different from soaps. Both are able to emulsify oils, hold dirt in suspension, and act as wetting agents. Since the 1950s, some soaps have included detergents, which work better than soap in hard water. (Soap combines with the minerals in hard water, leaving a bathtub ring; detergents do not tend to form such scum.) Most liquid products are basically detergent, not soap.

You can wash your hands for a penny with most soaps, but some designer brands cost around 4 or 5 cents per wash. Here's what a soap maker can do to make a penny's wash seem worth a nickel, a dime, or a quarter:

■ *Add fancy perfume.* In its natural state, soap smells somewhat like the fat in fresh meat. Fragrance masks this odor. Some soap makers think that if they mask the odor well enough, it will upscale their product from the supermarket shelf—where soap can cost a dollar or less per bar—to the beauty counter at department stores, where you can easily pay $10 a bar.

■ *Appeal to health.* The package may claim that the soap is "hypoallergenic" or "noncomedogenic" (that means the soap won't clog pores and promote blackheads, or comedones). A manufacturer makes formulations for different skin types.

■ *Promise beauty.* Manufacturers pledge that added emollients—

bath oil, moisturizing cream, lanolin, vitamin E—will soften and condition skin. (As the Better Business Bureau reports, no soap can be truthfully represented to keep skin young, and none may be advertised "as a cure, remedy, or competent treatment" for any skin disease.)

■ *Prevent embarrassment.* Some brands claim that they are able to keep body odor at bay. These deodorant soaps usually include an antibacterial agent. (Perspiration itself doesn't smell. Body odor is caused by bacteria that act on perspiration.) All provide protection against unwanted odors because all soaps float off bacteria along with dirt and grease.

PERFORMANCE

Consumers Union found that all soaps tested by a panel were at least good in cleaning or in the way they left hands feeling, but some clearly performed better than others. Liquids generally didn't feel as good on the skin as bar soap, probably because they are more likely to contain detergent, which tends to feel harsher than soap.

Soap and detergent can dry the skin because they remove its natural oils. Once its oil coating is gone, the skin readily gives up water. Most soaps have emollients, which may help seal in moisture.

If you have dry skin, however, don't look for some magic soap formula to provide relief. Apply baby oil or a moisturizer after bathing, while the skin is still damp.

COST

It makes no sense to pay more than a penny a wash for soap. On average, liquid soaps are slightly more expensive to use than bars, and their plastic containers often leave more packaging waste. (For many liquids, a pump refill is available, but then the refill bottle is tossed out.)

TOILET TISSUES

Whatever the price per roll, you expect certain basic qualities in this homely but indispensable product.

The stronger the tissue when wet, the less likely it is to break or tear in use. Wet strength is far more important than dry strength. Two-ply tissues are stronger as a group, but there are some strong single-plies, too.

Most toilet tissues are soft enough for all but sensitive individuals. Many people won't find even the roughest toilet tissues objectionable. Two-ply tissues are generally softer than single-ply.

Toilet tissues should quickly and thoroughly absorb moisture. When last tested, two-ply models soaked up a drop of water within five seconds or less. Most single-ply tissues were not quite as absorbent.

Tissues should break up promptly when flushed away. If they don't, a slow toilet may back up.

Some tissues are scented. Scent serves no practical purpose in bathroom tissues, and it may be irritating to some people.

CONVENIENCE

Some tissues come in single rolls, some in packages of 12 or more. Four-packs are the most popular.

A package should be easy to open, the roll should be easy to start, and tissues should be easy to tear off. Plastic packages with perforations around the top are easiest to open.

On some rolls, the first few sheets stick to the ones underneath, an annoyance when you begin using the roll. On others, the end of the first sheet hangs free, providing a pull tab that's easy to grasp. Sometimes the tab works well; sometimes it shreds before freeing the next sheet.

Most two-ply models are relatively easy to detach, thanks to their adequate perforations. By contrast, some single-ply products are flimsy and tend to tear raggedly.

SUMMARY

No tissues have all four qualities: softness, strength, ability to tear easily, and inexpensiveness. Some qualities are mutually exclusive. For example, softness generally doesn't go with strength. Then again, perhaps all the fuss about softness is unnecessary.

Appendix A

TIPS FOR CLEANING
A VARIETY OF HOUSEHOLD ITEMS

Acetate fabric. Dry cleaning is safest for this delicate fabric even if there are laundering instructions on the care label. Hand laundering must be carefully done. Avoid wringing or twisting garments. Dry acetate items by carefully spreading them out on terry-cloth bath towels on a horizontal surface or draping them over a clothesline. Do not use nail polish remover or other cleaners that contain acetone to attempt to remove stains. Acetone will dissolve acetate.

Acrylic furniture. Gently dust acrylic furniture with a damp cloth or chamois. Wash with hand dishwashing liquid and water using a soft cloth. Rinse with water and blot dry with a clean cloth.

Air conditioners. Clean or change a window air conditioner's filter once a month during the air-conditioning season to keep the machine's efficiency as high as possible. When cleaning or changing the filter, vacuum clean any visible cooling coils. (Be careful not to cut yourself on sharp edges.) Plastic foam filters can be washed at the kitchen sink, using a mild solution of a hand dishwashing liquid and water. Condenser coils facing outside also need cleaning before hot weather sets in, but the unit may have to be removed from the window to do the job. In very sooty areas, or when the air conditioner is in a window over a heavily trafficked street, you may need to hire a professional firm to do the cleaning.

Aluminum cookware. Acidic foods—such as tomatoes or rhubarb—may remove stains or discolorations as they are being cooked. You can also boil a solution of one quart of water containing 2 to 3 tablespoons of vinegar or lemon juice in the cookware, followed by light rubbing with a soap-filled scouring pad.

Aluminum scuffs. Some porcelain sinks, especially older ones with a bit of their enamel worn off, tend to collect scuff marks from aluminum pots and pans. A good cleanser should readily remove these marks. Cover the stain with the cleanser for a few minutes, then rinse it off.

Appliance exteriors. Many kitchen and laundry appliances have a baked enamel surface that scratches easily, unlike the glass-hard porcelain enamel finish that is common on kitchen ranges as well as on some washing machines or other appliance tops. Never use an abrasive cleaner on baked enamel. Hand dishwashing liquid and water should do the job. If this doesn't work, a liquid all-purpose cleaner can help, but check the label instructions to be sure the manufacturer states that it is safe to use on painted surfaces.

Asphalt tile. Damp mop for day-to-day cleaning. Don't use solvent-based wax; the solvent can soften and damage the tile.

Audiotape recording and playback heads. It is important to periodically clean recording and playback heads, capstans, pinch rollers, and tape guides. Once a month is probably a reasonable interval. Use a small cotton swab or—even better—a lint-free piece of cotton cloth wrapped around the swab. The swab or cloth should be lightly moistened with cleaning agent. You can use rubbing alcohol (isopropyl alcohol), but it is probably safer and better to buy tape-head cleaner from an electronics supply store. If the deck or tape player is not accessible for cleaning, you might try a special head-cleaning tape. Carefully follow instructions. Never use any kind of abrasive material to clean the heads.

Auto carpeting, upholstery, and mats. Regular vacuuming is important to prevent buildup of particulate matter that can contribute to carpet wear. A plug-in, lightweight, handheld vacuum cleaner works best. A cordless model with rechargeable batteries may work well enough on loose surface litter.

Barbecue grills. If you run a gas barbecue for about 15 minutes at the highest heat setting—after you finish cooking—it should look reasonably clean but may still need some wire brushing to get rid of any heavy residue. When using a charcoal barbecue, let the grill stand over the coals for about 20 minutes after cooking to achieve similar results. Any remaining baked-on dirt should yield to wire brushing or to an abrasive powdered cleaner.

Bath mats. Many bath mats and toilet tank covers can be cleaned in a washing machine. Use a mild detergent at a setting of not more than 90°F for dark colors and 105°F for light colors or whites, rinse thoroughly, and tumble dry using a low temperature setting. In lieu of machine drying, hang or spread items in the shade until dry, then brush lightly.

Bathroom fixtures. Some bathroom cleaners can mar brass, paint, stainless steel, vinyl shower curtains, or wallpaper. Immediately rinse off cleaner to avoid damage.

Blankets. Read and follow the manufacturer's care instructions. For best results, wash each blanket separately. Be sure the blanket dries evenly. Nonwoven blankets contain synthetic fibers that are pressed together and heat bonded. They should be machine washed with a gentle cycle, using warm water and a high water level, then air dried. Vellux nonwoven blankets use adhesives to bond the fibers to a foam base. They should be washed using a short agitation cycle of five to eight minutes. Vellux blankets can be tumble dried at low heat. Wool blankets should be machine washed in cold water on the delicate cycle; tumble dry on low heat.

Blenders. Glass containers stay better-looking longer than plastic ones because they resist scratching and staining; a glass container should be dishwasher safe. A plastic container probably should not go into a dishwater, as it might soften or melt if placed too close to the machine's heating element. As an alternative to hand washing, fill with water, add a few drops of hand dishwashing liquid, cover, and blend the solution on the Stir setting for 10 to 20 seconds or until the sides are clean; then rinse thoroughly.

Brass. Lacquered brass should be cleaned only with hand dishwashing liquid and water. Anything stronger may ruin the finish. Clean unlacquered brass with a commercial copper or brass cleaner, then wash in sudsy water and rinse. Buff with a soft clean cloth.

Butcher blocks. See *Wooden work surfaces*.

Camcorders. To clean the lens surface, first blow off dust with a blower brush. Then, to remove any smudges or fingerprints, gently wipe the lens surface with a piece of lens cleaning paper or a clean cotton cloth moistened with a drop or two of lens-cleaning fluid (available at camera stores). Clean in a spiral motion from the center outward.

A noisy picture during playback can be caused by an incorrectly set tracking control, by clogged video heads, or by a circuit failure. Preferably, video head cleaning should be performed by a qualified service technician. An alternate solution is to use a head-cleaning cassette—but only when necessary. Cautiously use the cleaning cassette in strict accordance with the manufacturer's instructions. If the cleaning tape doesn't restore the picture in a few tries, professional servicing may be necessary.

Cameras. To clean the lens surface, first blow off dust with a blower brush. Then, to remove any smudges or fingerprints, gently wipe the lens surface with a piece of lens cleaning paper or a clean cotton cloth moistened with a drop or two of lens-cleaning fluid (available at camera stores). Clean in a spiral motion from the center outward.

Caution: Do not use film cleaner. It contains organic solvents that may damage the lens or camera finish.

With proper care, the mirror and focusing screen in an SLR camera should stay clean enough. If cleaning becomes necessary, use a blower brush. If more cleaning is necessary, *never* attempt to do it yourself. Take the camera to an authorized service facility.

Use a blower brush to remove accumulated film dust particles from the film chamber, being careful not to touch the shutter. Store the blower brush in a container or plastic bag to keep it clean.

Carpet grit. Use a full-size upright vacuum cleaner or canister model with a power nozzle. Vacuum on a regular basis. This is especially important near entrance doors and in heavily traveled areas.

Cat litter box. Use hot water and hand dishwasher liquid to clean litter box surfaces. Avoid using chlorine bleach for cleaning: Fumes are created through a chemical reaction between the bleach and residual ammonia remaining in a litter box after it has been emptied.

China dishware. It's best to wash fine china by hand with a hand dishwashing liquid. Some dishwasher detergents may wear away the overglaze and metallic decorations on some fine china, and fine china can easily be chipped or broken by forceful water jets or jostling among pots and pans. Everyday china can be washed in the dishwasher.

Citrus juicers. The easiest-to-clean juicer has the cone, strainer, and juice container as a single unit. Models with several pieces have to be taken apart, washed, dried, and put back together. It's helpful if the pieces can be put into a dishwasher; check the manufacturer's instructions.

Clothes dryers. Clean a dryer's lint screen after each load. This will maintain high drying efficiency and will help to prevent excessive heat buildup. Vacuum clean any visible lint buildup in other parts of the machine, but leave any disassembling to a service technician.

Coffeemakers. The carafe and brew basket of a drip-type coffeemaker should be cleaned after every use because dried coffee oils can ruin the taste of even the best blend. Coffee taste may also be improved by using a special coffeemaker cleaner. Because minerals accumulate in the tank and tubes of automatic-drip units, it's important to clean them now and then, especially if they are used with hard water. As a substitute for a commercial cleaner, try running white vinegar diluted with water through the machine. It's a chore, but worth the trouble.

Compact discs (CDs). Light dust will not harm a CD. Heavier dust can be removed by gentle strokes with a soft, lint-free cloth. Always wipe the CD in the radial direction—across the "grooves." Radial scratches will be ignored by the CD player. Smudges or deposits should be washed off under running water with a little hand dishwashing liquid if needed; then rinse the CD, allow the excess water to run off and carefully pat it dry with a soft lint-free cloth.

Computer keyboards. Vacuum keyboards regularly, using the soft brush attachment. To dislodge particles of dirt and dust, turn the keyboard upside down and hit it several times with the flat of your hand. You can also use a can of compressed air (available from electronics stores). Periodically, clean the keys with either a lint-free cloth dipped in rubbing alcohol or a commercial keyboard wipe. Be sure to unplug the keyboard first, or shut the computer off.

Computer monitors. See *Television sets*.

Concrete floors. Many methods recommended for removing stains from concrete involve use of strong solvents like trisodium phosphate or flammable materials like kerosene, and lots of elbow grease. Because of safety concerns, Consumers Union cannot recommend a home brew for this purpose. However, there are some commercially available products that may do the job. It is extremely important to read and carefully follow the directions and safety precautions when using these products.

Continuous-cleaning ovens. The porous finish of a continuous-cleaning oven is supposed to dissipate light dirt gradually at normal cooking temperatures. But major spills won't go away—you have to wipe them up right after they happen. Minor spills appear to be eliminated slowly, partly because they spread out on the finish, which is mottled, thereby helping to disguise patches of dirt. You can protect most exposed surfaces from becoming soiled in the first place by covering the oven bottom with aluminum foil, but be careful to avoid blocking any vents in a gas oven or short-circuiting an electric element.

Copper cookware. Clean with a commercial copper cleaner, then wash in sudsy water and rinse. Buff with a soft clean cloth.

Countertops. A quick wipe with a damp cloth or with a cloth containing a mild solution of hand dishwashing liquid will take care of most spills on laminated countertops. Be sure to remove any puddles immediately, to avoid warping. Never use an abrasive cleanser on a plastic-laminate surface. For more difficult stains, clean these easy-to-scratch surfaces with the gentlest all-purpose cleaner possible, rinse thoroughly, and dry with a soft cloth. For very stubborn spots (like newsprint ink), use undiluted liquid household bleach, being sure to follow the label directions for proper use. Let the bleach stand for no more than 1½ minutes and then rinse thoroughly with warm water. In the bathroom, liquid cleaners should be rinsed off to prevent damage to the countertop finish.

Curtains. Vacuum thin fabrics at a reduced suction setting to prevent the fabric from being drawn into the cleaner's nozzle. It might be helpful to place a stiff piece of plastic screen between the nozzle and the fabric, to prevent the fabric from being sucked into the nozzle.

Dehumidifiers. Vacuum the coils at least once a year, more often in a dusty environment. This will help maintain the appliance's performance.

Delicate fabrics. Follow the manufacturer's care and cleaning instructions. The less time some delicate fabrics spend in water, even cold water, the better.

Dish sanitizing. Some dishwashers have a final rinse cycle that uses extra-hot water. Their makers claim that this helps prevent the spread of cold and flu germs. In fact, once you put "sanitized" dishes into the cupboard, household microbes—the same microbes that are on everything else in the house—quickly settle on them.

Disinfecting. It's really not possible to prevent the spread of germs in the house by using a disinfectant. When a medical problem arises that requires using a germicide, ask a doctor for advice on how to proceed.

Dust on hard surfaces. A little bit of spray furniture polish on a rag makes the rag tacky enough to pick up more dust than a dry cloth.

Electric blankets. Follow the manufacturer's instructions for laundering (usually a cold or warm wash and low-heat machine drying or, even better, line drying). Never have an electric blanket or pad dry-cleaned; dry-cleaning chemicals can damage the wiring. Do not machine-dry unless the care label recommends it. Instead, hang the blanket over two clotheslines or lay it flat to dry.

Electric range tops. Electric coil elements are all self-cleaning, since spills burn off quickly. If you soak an electric element in water, it may become damaged. Clean under the control knobs by pulling them off. Use care when scrubbing around the control panel: The markings can often be rubbed off with steel wool or an abrasive powdered cleanser.

You can raise or remove the cooktop to clean beneath it. But some electric ranges have a fixed cooktop; in that case, you have to poke your hand through the burner holes. Clean drip pans and reflector bowls with the least abrasive cleanser that will keep them looking up to par. A new spare set of drip pans or reflectors is handy for making the cooktop presentable at a moment's notice.

Smooth-top cooktops should be cleaned with a special cleaner made for such use. Spills of food—especially those containing sugar—should be wiped up immediately.

Fans. Dirty fan blades impair air-moving efficiency and also detract from the appliance's appearance. Clean metal blades carefully to prevent bending them, which can cause unwanted vibration when the fan is turned on. A whole-house or attic fan's louvers and screening should be brushed and vacuumed at least once a season to keep the air-flow rate at the maximum.

Floor cleaning. A lightweight upright vacuum cleaner works well for picking up loose dirt from bare floors. For stains and adherent soil, however, use a damp (not wet) sponge mop or its equivalent.

Floor wax buildup. Try a wax remover. Use fine steel wool for stubborn spots.

Food processors. The simple, clean lines of these machines make for easy cleaning. Use a damp sponge for gaps around switches and trim.

Freezers. Self-defrosting is available in some upright models: You can skip the manual defrosting chore and just swab down inside surfaces with a cleaning solution of baking soda (bicarbonate of soda) and water.

A chest freezer has a smooth interior and removable wire baskets or dividers instead of shelves. Use a windshield ice scraper to remove frost and hasten defrosting. An upright freezer requires more patience because you must wait for the ice to melt off the cooling coils in the shelves. If you use a tool to scrape and pry ice away to speed the process, the result could be damage to the refrigeration system, which is expensive to repair.

Defrost when the food supply is low. Transfer any remaining food to an iced picnic chest or to the refrigerator's freezer or cooling compartment. Or wrap food in food wrap, then layers of newspaper for insulation while you defrost. On a very cold winter day, you may be able to store the food outdoors while you defrost.

Furniture. The original oil or lacquer finish on a piece of furniture provides the best protection. Quickly clean up spills before they have a chance to attack the finish. Use the softest cloth possible for dusting.

If you apply polish each time you dust, excessive wax buildup can result, causing loss of the wood's natural beauty as well as difficulty in getting the kind of luster you really want. Don't wipe against the grain. Be sure to use soft insulating pads under hot, heavy, or sharp objects or containers.

Furniture nicks and scratches. Some polishes are colored to match the furniture wood, and thereby mask the marred area, but the color match must be accurate for the cover-up to work well.

Garbage disposers. Most manufacturers suggest allowing a disposer to run for 30 to 60 seconds after grinding is finished. Some also suggest purging the disposer by filling the sink halfway with water, removing the drain stopper, and turning on the machine for a few seconds.

Glass-fiber fabrics. This material is resistant to soiling and can be very decorative. It is fragile and should be carefully hand-laundered and line dried.

Glassware. It is best to wash crystal glassware by hand; there's a possibility of chipping and breakage if you wash such items in a machine. Some glassware can become etched as a result of a chemical reaction of water, glassware, and detergent in a dishwasher. This phenomenon is especially prevalent in soft or softened water. Etching is irreversible. To minimize it, use a small amount of detergent and do not exceed 140°F water temperature. Underload the dishwasher to permit proper rinsing and draining, and dry without heat.

Greasy dirt on hard surfaces. Pine oil in some all-purpose cleaners helps penetrate and loosen greasy dirt.

Heaters. Some space heaters have shiny reflecting surfaces to help direct the heat where you want it. If the shiny area becomes dulled, the heater will be less effective. After unplugging the appliance, vacuum any surfaces you can reach.

Heating systems. Vacuum radiators and fins regularly during the heating season to keep them at their maximum operating efficiency. Change or wash any filters in a warm-air heating system at least once during the heating season, as well as during the summer if the air ducts also serve as part of a central air-conditioning system.

Hot plates. Unplug before cleaning. Do not immerse in water. Clean nonburner surfaces with warm water and hand dishwashing liquid and a dishcloth, sponge, or plastic scouring pad. For difficult-to-remove soil, use a fine soapy metal scouring pad. Be sure to test it first on an inconspicuous area.

Humidifier dust. If you use a cool mist or ultrasonic humidifier, you may be forever wiping up white dust that settles on furniture and other surfaces, even beyond the room in which the humidifier is located. If you live in a hard-water area, use only distilled water or demineralized water in cool-mist or ultrasonic humidifiers.

Humidifiers. Molds and bacteria from humidifiers and vaporizers may trigger allergic symptoms. Although ultrasonic models do not emit fine microorganisms, they have been implicated in spraying fragments of bacteria and molds into the air. Therefore, like cool-mist and evaporative humidifiers, an ultrasonic humidifier should be scrupulously cleaned daily.

After unplugging and emptying the humidifier, clean it as directed by the manufacturer. If there are no directions, rinse the tank with a solution of one tablespoon of chlorine bleach in a pint of water, followed by a thorough rinsing with fresh water. For large units, use a cup of bleach in a gallon of water, then rinse the tank thoroughly with fresh water.

A steam vaporizer, the kind that boils water and produces moisture in the form of steam, doesn't present problems of molds and bacteria. But a steam vaporizer must still be cleaned to keep it working properly. Rust or scale accumulations in a steam vaporizer are harmless but should be rinsed out periodically, particularly before storing the unit.

Insect killers ("bug zappers"). First unplug the appliance. It's usually difficult to poke through the outer screen or blow through it with a vacuum cleaner's exhaust. It's much easier to disassemble the unit, at least to the extent of removing the sides so that the grid can be brushed off properly.

Linen. This is a durable fabric whose appearance and "feel" improve with laundering. Linen that has been chemically treated for wrinkle resistance may withstand hot-water washing.

Lint on garments. A washing machine's lint filter helps, but tumbling in a clothes dryer may be even more effective. It's worth trying a lint roller or even wrapping Scotch-type sticky tape around a hand, sticky side out, and patting the garment to remove the lint.

Litter on carpeting and hard-surface floors. Use a lightweight vacuum cleaner. Reserve uprights and power brushes for cleaning deep in a carpet's pile.

Microwave cookware. Except for the browning dishes and the crevices on some trivets, cleaning microwave cookware should be easy with just hand dishwashing liquid and water. Some plastic utensils have a nonstick finish. This is usually unnecessary, since stuck-on food is seldom a problem in microwave cooking. The nonstick finishes are probably a drawback because they easily scratch and quickly look worn. Browning dishes sear food and accumulate a fair amount of burned-on soil that requires some cleaning effort to remove.

Microwave ovens. Wipe the inside with plain water, or water with a bit of hand dishwashing liquid. Spills and spatters are generally easy to wipe up with a damp (not wet) sponge. Keep the oven clean to prevent odors from developing.

Mildew around the house. Mildew has an unpleasant odor and appearance. It's a common household mold that thrives in dark, damp, poorly ventilated places. Chlorine bleach, diluted according to label directions, is a good mildew remover for use on colorfast, waterproof hard surfaces.

Mildew can also be controlled by lowering the humidity in a closed-in space such as a closet. In very humid weather, when mildew growth is greatest, use a continuously burning 60-watt bulb in a large closet to raise the temperature (and thereby lower the relative humidity). A smaller bulb can be used in a smaller enclosure. Be certain that the bulb is well away from any stored articles.

Mildew in bathrooms. Some specialty bathroom cleaners contain effective mildew fighters. But liquid chlorine bleach applied according to label directions is an effective mildew cleaner. Because it can discolor many fabrics and wallpaper, rinse thoroughly any mildewed surface that has been washed with bleach. Never mix bleach with other cleaning products. Bleach reacts with many household cleaners and can produce hazardous fumes.

Nylon. White nylon items should be washed separately because of nylon's tendency to pick up colors from other items in a laundry load. Oily substances can stick to nylon. Quickly rinse off these stains before they have a chance to set.

Ovens. Refer to the Oven Cleaners section in the chapter on House Cleaning, and *Continuous-cleaning ovens* and *Self-cleaning ovens* in this section.

Painted surfaces. All-purpose cleaners should be tried on an inconspicuous area first. Cleaners containing pine oil can damage paint. Avoid excessive rubbing and abrasive cleaning.

Polyester. Fabrics containing polyester fibers have a strong affinity for oily substances. Wash oily stains as soon as you notice them. Try rubbing them with a wet bar of hand soap, then with a wet towel followed by rinsing. Unfortunately, even quick attention may not result in satisfactory stain removal.

Porcelain enamel bathroom fixtures. Sinks, bathtubs, toilets, and other plumbing fixtures are generally made of metal with a heavy outside layer of glasslike porcelain. Porcelain can tolerate abrasive cleansers without wearing off, but the shiny finish will be gradually destroyed, making the fixture less resistant to staining and therefore more difficult to clean. Stick to nonabrasive cleansers on new or nearly new fixtures.

Porcelain enamel kitchen fixtures. Treat these items as gently as possible to avoid unsightly scratches that can make future cleaning increasingly difficult.

Portable food mixers. Crevices and grooves trap food and dirt. A dampened new toothbrush reserved for this purpose can help.

Rayon. See *Silk.*

Records, long-playing (LP). Keeping an LP record dust-free is the best way to make it last longer. Records should be cleaned immediately before you play them with a cloth-pile brush available from an electronics store. Handle records only by their edges to prevent perspiration and skin oils from attaching dust to the record's surfaces. When putting a record away, make sure the opening in the inner sleeve doesn't coincide with the opening in the outer cover. Be sure any commercial record-cleaning spray you might purchase does not contain silicone, which can cause dust to stick to records.

Refrigerator/freezers. The condenser coil, which helps disperse heat, is outside the cabinet, where it tends to collect dust. Dust lowers the appliance's efficiency and raises the cost of running it. The condenser should be cleaned once or twice a year, particularly before the onset of hot weather, because high outside temperatures impose heavy demands on a refrigerating system.

It's easy to clean a back-mounted condenser once you pull out the refrigerator. But in many models, the coil is mounted in a compartment underneath the cabinet. Clean this area by using a condenser-coil cleaning brush (available in hardware and appliance stores) and a vacuum cleaner's crevice tool. Most manufacturers tell you to clean from the front, a task made more difficult if the coil is under a shield and toward the refrigerator's back. Cleaning the coil from the back after you remove the cardboard "service access" cover is a bit easier, but you'll have to wrestle the appliance from its normal position.

Some older refrigerators have a removable drip pan that can develop odors from food spills that drip into it from inside the refrigerator. If possible, check it from time to time, and wash and rinse the pan using hand dishwashing liquid and water.

Cleaning inside the refrigerator is best done with the mildest possible detergent or just a damp sponge. Try to avoid scratching soft plastic surfaces. A solution of baking soda and water is probably enough to do the job if water alone doesn't work. It's particularly important to keep the door seal (gasket) clean: Dirt buildup impairs the gasket's ability to hold in the cold air.

Resin furniture. A soft cloth and all-purpose, nonabrasive cleaner will keep resin furniture clean for a long time.

Self-cleaning ovens. Use the self-cleaning cycle as often as necessary. The energy cost (using national average rates) is less per cleaning than an application of a chemical cleaner in an oven without the self-cleaning feature.

The self-cleaning cycle turns the most stubborn spills into a powdery gray ash residue. At the end of the cycle, simply wipe off the residue.

The self-cleaning cycle produces smoke and fumes, which exit through a vent on the back guard of gas models or under a rear element of electric ovens. If there's a loose duct from the oven to the rear element, hard-to-clean dirt may be deposited under the cook top during the cleaning cycle. Ventilate the kitchen during the self-cleaning cycle to prevent smoke and fume particles from being deposited on the kitchen's walls and ceiling.

A self-cleaning oven's door and frame usually need some scrubbing outside the door seal, where vaporized soil can leak through. Use the mildest nonabrasive cleanser. Avoid scrubbing the gasket itself, except very gently with a sponge that has been dampened with a solution of hand dishwashing liquid, followed by a sponge rinse with plain water.

Shavers. Men's electric shavers need daily cleaning. Unclip the blade cover. Shake and brush clippings from the cutters and the underside of the head. Once every week or two, the shaver should be cleaned thoroughly to help maintain its ability to operate satisfactorily, a job that usually involves removing, brushing, and refitting the cutters and the head.

Silk. Garments made of silk usually require dry cleaning because water and silk are often not compatible. However, there are some silk garments that can tolerate washing in water. Be guided by care labels. Some dyes used on silk will dissolve in water, causing dye bleeding and dye transfer. Be sure to test multicolored articles before washing.

Slow cookers. Avoid an abrasive cleaner or steel wool in favor of a sponge, cloth, or nonscratching plastic scrubber. Cleanup is easiest if the appliance has a removable liner that can be immersed. If the liner is not removable, take care not to wet any electrical parts of the cooker.

Smoke detectors. To keep detectors operating properly, vacuum them annually, cleaning with the vacuum wand from a full-powered canister cleaner, if possible. If a detector has a fixed cover, pass the wand across the cover's openings. If a detector's cover is removable, gently vacuum the sensor chambers.

Spots on glassware and dishes. This is a particularly annoying problem in areas of the country that have hard water. Try adding a rinse agent to your dishwashing machine. These products help to reduce spotting. Many dishwashers have dispensers for such additives.

Stainless steel cookware. For stubborn food residues, use a commercial stainless steel cleaner.

Stainless steel flatware. Scratches or surface imperfections tend to diminish the stain resistance of stainless steel tableware. Consequently, flatware should not be cleaned with scouring powder or steel wool. It is advisable to wash stainless steel soon after using it to minimize any possible staining.

Steam irons. Unplug the iron and allow it to cool down before cleaning. If an iron's soleplate has a nonstick finish, any adherent starch or dirt should be removed easily by wiping with a damp sponge. For an iron without a nonstick finish, clean with a mild solution of hand dishwashing liquid and water. Avoid abrasives, which could scratch the soleplate. Do not immerse the iron in water.

Television sets and computer monitors. A television's screen attracts fingerprints, but even more of a nuisance is its tendency to accumulate dust and grime as a result of static electricity. With the set turned off, use glass cleaner sparingly. Wet a rag or paper towel with the cleaner rather than spraying it, to avoid getting cleaner on the cabinet.

Toasters, toaster ovens, toaster oven–broilers. Clean the crumbs from these appliances often enough to prevent an accumulation that will smolder. Too many crumbs may also impede the operation of door-opening mechanisms.

A "continuous-clean" interior is supposed to rid itself of grease and grime at normal cooking temperatures. This doesn't seem to work very well, however, although a continuous-clean finish's dull, usually mottled surface may present a cleaner appearance for a longer time than an ordinary finish will. In the long run, a continuous-clean finish may be something of a disadvantage since its rough, soft surface eventually makes cleaning very difficult. It doesn't hold up to scrubbing or to the use of harsh cleansers.

Vacuum cleaners. Clumps of dust or other debris can clog a vacuum cleaner's hose. One way to dislodge dirt is with a broom or mop handle inserted into the hose, working carefully to prevent puncturing the hose cover. Change the paper bag or clean the cloth bag as soon as the cleaner's suction drops noticeably, even if the bag doesn't seem full. Small quantities of fine, dense dirt can reduce a bag's efficiency and consequently a cleaner's suction.

Vaporizers. See *Humidifiers.*

VCR recording and playback heads. The picture generated by a VCR may begin to deteriorate over time. Replacing the heads can be expensive. There is not much you can do about normal wear resulting from the head spinning at high speed against the tape and the tape moving past the head. Try to keep the machine as free of dust as possible by covering it when the VCR is not in use and by storing tapes where they aren't likely to gather a lot of dust and debris. You might try a special VCR cleaning tape, cautiously using it in strict accordance with the manufacturer's instructions. If the cleaning tape doesn't restore the picture, professional servicing may be necessary.

Vinyl and vinyl-composition floors. Damp mop for day-to-day cleaning.

Waffle makers. The bits of food that stick to nonstick grids can be removed with a brush when the grids are cool. When you want to wash away excess oil, dunk removable grids in a sinkful of warm, sudsy water. (*Never* dunk the appliance itself.) Flat grids for grilling usually require thorough cleaning—sometimes soaking—to remove hamburger grease or sticky cheese. Many manufacturers recommend washing the grids by hand rather than in a dishwasher.

Washing machines. Follow the manufacturer's instructions for cleaning underneath the agitator or cleaning a lint filter. Sponge off detergent accumulations from around the top of the machine.

Water heaters. Periodically drain off some hot water to keep sediment from accumulating at the bottom of the tank. In areas with hard water, draining is best done every month. Where the water is soft, every three or four months should be enough. Be aware that sometimes after this is done, sediment gets caught in the drain valve, which will leak.

Wooden work surfaces. Butcher blocks and other wooden work surfaces used for food preparation should be cleaned after each use. Use chlorine bleach to kill germs from raw foods such as chicken, fish, and meat. Wash any surface that touches these foods. Then cover the surface for two minutes with a dilute solution of unscented chlorine bleach, rinse thoroughly, and air dry.

Wood-handled utensils. Unless the manufacturer's instructions say the utensil is dishwasher safe, it is better to hand wash it in hot, soapy water and towel dry. Do not allow the utensil to soak in the water. Doing so may damage the wood.

Wool. Dry cleaning is the safest method, unless the item has a care label stating that it is machine washable. If it says the wool can be laundered, use only cool or cold water, and use minimum agitation and spinning to prevent shrinkage and matting of the wool fibers. Do not use bleach.

Appendix B

STAIN REMOVAL

Quick action is often the key to success with stain removal. Many a tie, blouse, carpet, or upholstery fabric has been saved by immediately treating the stain. Gather all of the materials mentioned in the section entitled "Spot Removal Kit" (see p. 182) and keep them in a place where you can locate them quickly. Be sure they are out of the reach of children.

It is important to follow the garment, carpet, or furniture manufacturer's instructions as well as the cautions listed on the label of any product used in the stain removal process. The process of attempting to remove a stain may be unsuccessful and may, in fact, set the stain, making it more difficult to remove. If you are not sure if your attempt to remove a stain will cause damage, it might be better to seek professional help (a dry cleaner or a professional carpet, drapery, or upholstery cleaning service). But it is important to understand that even though professional cleaning may do the trick, it too is not always a foolproof approach. Professionals may not be able to remove some stains. Be sure the professional you select evaluates the stain and the stained material, and informs you about any potential risks associated with attempting to remove the stain.

Cleaning procedures. The following procedures have been obtained from several sources, including the Association of Specialists in Cleaning and Restoration (ASCR International) and the Carpet and Rug Institute (CRI). Neither the editors nor the publisher can guarantee or be responsible for any results obtained by using these procedures.

Whether you plan to attempt stain removal yourself or use the services of a professional, it is important to blot up all spills immediately using clean, white unprinted napkins or towels. You may use cloth or paper for this purpose. However, if you decide to use paper napkins or towels, first test them to be sure they will be strong enough to do the job.

Do not scrub the area! Scrubbing can damage delicate fabrics or carpet pile. Continue to blot with napkins or towels until the area is completely dry. For semi-solids, gently scrape the residue up with the edge of a rounded spoon. On carpets, solids should be gently broken up and vacuumed until completely removed.

For any residual stain resulting from a spill or for stains that have already had a chance to soak into the fabric and dry, locate the substance that caused the stain in the stain removal steps section (see p. 184) and carefully follow the recommended cleaning steps in the order shown.

Pretest each recommended cleaning agent on an inconspicuous area of the soiled item (inside the flap that covers a zipper, under or in back of a couch cushion, the back of a tie, a section of carpet inside a closet, etc.) using the following pretest procedure. On a multicolor fabric, conduct the test in a place where the different colors meet, or be sure to test each of the colors.

- Apply several drops of the cleaning agent to the testing area.
- Hold a wet white cloth on the testing area for 60 seconds. If you can get to both sides, do the same on the underside of the fabric.
- Examine the wet cloth for color transfer and the fabric or carpet for color change or damage. If any of these changes are evident, try the next cleaning solution in the recommended sequence or seek professional help.

If no damage or color change is evident from the pretest, you may begin the cleaning process. Apply a small amount of the first recommended cleaning agent to a white cloth or paper towel and gently work it into the stained area. Problems can result from working with large amounts of cleaning materials, even water. So it is better to start with a small amount of cleaning agent and repeat the process as needed. *Blot*—do not rub or brush. Excessive agitation can cause unsightly fabric or carpet pile distortion, which may become permanent. Work from the outer edge of the stain toward the center. Repeat the procedure with additional clean white cloths or paper towels until you can't transfer any more stain to the cloth or towel. Do not proceed to the next recommended cleaning agent until this is done. Be patient! Complete stain removal may require repeating the same step several times. In many cases it will not be necessary to use all of the recommended steps to remove the stain.

If you have access to the back of the fabric on clothing, place the front face on a white towel and work the cleaning agent into the fabric from the back. Of course, this is not typically possible when cleaning upholstery or carpets.

Some cleaning agents may promote rapid resoiling. For washable clothing, launder the garment as soon as possible after removing the stain. For fabrics or carpet materials that are water safe, it is also important to rinse or wash the area after the stain has been removed completely. During the process of rinsing, avoid using excessive amounts of water on carpets and upholstery fabrics. Use a mist-type sprayer to prevent overwetting. For those nonwashable fabrics that will tolerate water, the treated fabric should be damp-sponged with cool water to remove any residue from the stain removal process. Check a garment's care label; if it reads "Dry Clean Only," you may want to avoid using water-based cleaning agents. Likewise, upholstery fabrics that carry a label with an "S" (indicating that a solvent-based cleaner is required) or an "X" (vacuuming only) should not be cleaned with any materials that contain water. Occasionally, professional cleaners have special techniques to clean upholstery labeled "X." They usually charge extra for this work. Upholstery cleaning codes are not always attached to furniture: Check the underside of a chair or sofa or look on the deck under the cushions.

After the stain is removed from a carpet or upholstery fabric and the area has been rinsed, apply a thick pad of white cloth or paper towels and weight them down to absorb the excess water or cleaning material from the final cleaning step. Change pads as needed until the area is thoroughly dry.

Consumers Union testers found that some of the more effective laundry detergents (especially those with bleach or bleach alternative) were quite effective at removing stains caused by spaghetti sauce, chocolate milk, and mud. Most could not remove motor oil.

Worth Writing For

■ Contact the Carpet and Rug Institute (P.O. Box 2048, Dalton, GA 30722, 800-882-8846) for a copy of their Carpet Spot Removal Guide.

■ If you have small children, contact Binney & Smith, Inc., Consumer Communications (P.O. Box 431, Easton, PA 18044, 1-800-CRAYOLA), for a copy of their Stain Removal Suggestions for *Crayola* products.

■ Write to ACR International (10830 Annapolis Junction Road, Suite 312, Annapolis Junction, MD 20701). Enclose a legal-size self-addressed stamped envelope for a copy of their carpet and upholstery spot removal guide.

■ Contact the Institute of Inspection, Cleaning and Restoration Certification (800-835-4624) and the Association of Specialists in

Cleaning and Restoration (800-272-7012) for listings of professional interior cleaners in your area.

OTHER ITEMS WORTH KEEPING AROUND

Baking soda. Can be used to neutralize acids (e.g., battery acid).
Bleach. Refer to the section on Bleaches in the Laundry chapter.
Hydrogen peroxide. The kind sold as an antiseptic (3 percent).
Petroleum jelly. Can be used to soften hardened paint, tar, and rubber cement on washable fabrics. (Launder fabrics treated with petroleum jelly immediately after application.)
Laundry booster. Refer to the section on Boosters in the Laundry chapter.

SPOT REMOVAL KIT

Use the recommended stain removal agents in the order indicated in the following table.

Dry cleaning. Some examples of nonflammable dry cleaning fluid are *Afta* and *K2r*. Use small amounts to avoid damage to sizing, backing, or stuffing material. Apply only in a well-ventilated area or—if possible—outdoors. (*Note:* The active ingredient in these products is being phased out by the EPA. Consumers Union does not know how the reformulated versions will perform.)

Detergent. (mild) Mix one teaspoon of a clear (not colored) hand dishwashing liquid per one cup of lukewarm water. Hand dishwashing liquid residues can cause rapid resoiling, so rinse thoroughly after using. Never use laundry detergents on upholstery or carpets because they contain optical brighteners that may discolor the fibers or affect light and white colors.

Ammonia. Mix 1 tablespoon of household ammonia with ½ cup of water.

Caution: Apply only in a well-ventilated area. Never mix ammonia and bleach during any cleaning operation.

Vinegar (5 percent acetic acid solution). Mix ⅓ cup of white household vinegar with ⅔ cup of water.

Enzyme. To make an enzyme-containing detergent, mix a solution of powdered enzyme-containing laundry detergent according to the directions on the box. Allow the solution to remain on the stain for the length of time recommended by the manufacturer.

Caution: Do not use an enzyme detergent on nonwashable fabrics, especially wool, mohair, or silk.

Alcohol. (Rubbing) Seventy-percent alcohol is available in most drug- and grocery stores.

Caution: Rubbing alcohol is ignitable. Use in a well-ventilated area, away from heat or flame, and store carefully.

Remover. Some nail polish removers contain acetone. Some may contain amyl acetate. Amyl acetate is also used in paint, oil, and grease (POG) removers (available in hardware stores). POG removers may leave residues that can cause rapid soiling. When using a POG remover on upholstery and carpets, always blot the area with a dry cleaning fluid, then rinse the area thoroughly with warm water. (See cautions for overwetting on p. 180.)

Caution: Do not attempt to clean acetate or triacetate fabrics with nail polish remover. Acetone and amyl acetate are ignitable.

Water. Rinsing with water alone should be the last step of the stain removal process. Do not overwet upholstery fabrics, carpets, and nonwashable clothing. Use a moist towel or a mist-type sprayer for gentle rinsing.

Professional. A professional should be called if an item is especially important to you, if you are in doubt with regard to the best stain removal method, or if there is a possibility that you'll damage the stained material. Professionals have the ability and the equipment to use more aggressive cleaning solutions to remove stubborn stains.

Vacuum. This is a handy tool for picking up loose dry spills.

Caution: Do not use gasoline or lighter fluid.

FOR STAIN REMOVAL, EMPLOY THE FOLLOWING STEPS IN THE ORDER PRESENTED (1=FIRST, 2=SECOND, ETC.).

Stain	Dry cleaning	Detergent	Ammonia	Vinegar	Enzyme	Alcohol
Acne medication	1					
Airplane cement	2	3				
Alcoholic beverages		1	2	3		
Animal stains		1	2	3		
Ashes						
Battery acid			1			
Beer		1	2	3	4	
Blood		2	1		3	
Butter	1	2	3	4		
Candle wax	2	3		4		
Candy		1	2	3		
Catsup		1	2	3	4	
Caulk, latex		1	2			

Use the recommended cleaning agents in the order indicated in the table. For more information, see page 182.
Dry cleaning = Nonflammable dry cleaning fluid. **Detergent** = mild detergent.

	Remover	Water	Professional	Vacuum	Comments
			2		Caution: Do not use water. Doing so may result in a permanent stain.
	1				—
					—
					—
			2	1	Masking tape can be substituted for vacuuming.
			2		First neutralize the acid with baking soda (sodium bicarbonate).
					—
					For washable clothing, pre-soaking for several hours in cold salt water may help. Full-strength 3% hydrogen peroxide may also help. Note: All cleaning agents should be used at room temperature (not warm or hot).
					—
	1 (POG)				Scrape excess wax off the fabric before cleaning. For washable clothing, pouring boiling water through the fabric from a height of 12 inches may help. For nonwashables, sandwich the fabric between paper towels and use a warm iron.
					—
					—
			3		—

Ammonia. **Vinegar**. **Enzyme** = Enzyme-containing detergent. **Alcohol** = Rubbing alcohol. **Remover** = Nail polish or POG remover. **Water**. **Professiona**l = Call a professional. **Vacuum**.

Stain	Dry cleaning	Detergent	Ammonia	Vinegar	Enzyme	Alcohol
Cheese	5	1	2	3	4	
Chewing gum	1	2				
Chicken soup	2	1				
Chocolate	5	1	2	3	4	
Coffee	5	1		2	4	
Coffee with cream and sugar	1	2		3	4	
Cola		1	2	3		
Copier toner						
Correction fluid	1					
Cosmetics	2	3	4	5		

Use the recommended cleaning agents in the order indicated in the table. For more information, see page 182.
Dry cleaning = Nonflammable dry cleaning fluid. **Detergent** = mild detergent.

Remover	Water	Professional	Vacuum	Comments
				—
		3		Freeze the gum with ice and gently break with a hammer to remove before cleaning. You can also rub about ½ tsp of full-strength liniment (e.g., *Ben-Gay*) into the affected area, heat the area with a hair dryer, and wipe with polyethylene squares. Follow with mild detergent and a rinse. For washables, softening the gum with peanut butter followed by laundering might facilitate removal. Caution: Peanut butter can also stain. Pretest before using this remedy.
				—
				Scrape off excess material before cleaning.
		3		For washable clothing, pouring boiling water through the fabric from a height of 12 inches may help.
				For washable clothing, pouring boiling water through the fabric from a height of 12 inches may help.
				—
		2	1	—
		2		Call the correction fluid manufacturer for suggested removal procedures.
1				—

Ammonia. Vinegar. Enzyme = Enzyme-containing detergent. **Alcohol** = Rubbing alcohol. **Remover** = Nail polish or POG remover. **Water. Professional** = Call a professional. **Vacuum.**

Stain	Dry cleaning	Detergent	Ammonia	Vinegar	Enzyme	Alcohol	
Crayon	1	2					
Diaper stains		1	2	3			
Dirt		2					
Driveway sealer							
Egg		1	2	3	4		
Eggnog	4	1		3			
Fecal matter		1	2	3			
Fruit & juices		1	2	3	4		
Fudge sauce	5	1	2	3	4		
Furniture stain	1	2					
Gasoline	1	2		3			
Glue, Elmer's		1					

Use the recommended cleaning agents in the order indicated in the table. For more information, see page 182.
Dry cleaning = Nonflammable dry cleaning fluid. **Detergent** = mild detergent.

Remover	Water	Professional	Vacuum	Comments
		3		Scrape off excess crayon before attempting stain removal. For washable clothing, pouring boiling water through the fabric from a height of 12 inches may help. When in doubt—for stains from crayon, tempera, and the like—call 1-800-CRAYOLA.
				—
	3		1	—
		1		—
				—
	2			—
				—
				For washable clothing, pouring boiling water through the fabric from a height of 12 inches may help. Consumers Union testers also found that several laundry booster products helped the removal of grape juice.
				—
		3		—
				On colorfast textiles, a dilute bleach solution may remove gasoline odor. Be sure to pretest before using this method.
	2	3		—

Ammonia. **Vinegar**. **Enzyme** = Enzyme-containing detergent. **Alcohol** = Rubbing alcohol. **Remover** = Nail polish or POG remover. **Water**. **Professional** = Call a professional. **Vacuum**.

Stain	Dry cleaning	Detergent	Ammonia	Vinegar	Enzyme	Alcohol	
Glue, white		2		1			
Grass	2	3	4	5	6		
Gravy	4	1	2	3			
Grease	1	2	3	4			
Greasy foods	1	2					
Hair dye		1	2	3			
Hair spray		1				3	
Hair tonic	1	2	3	4			
Ice cream	5	1	2	3	4		
Infant formula	2	1			3		
Ink, ballpoint	3	4	5	6		1	
Ink, fountain pen	1	2					
Ink, India	2	3					
Ink, marking pen		2				1	
Ink, permanent							

Use the recommended cleaning agents in the order indicated in the table. For more information, see page 182.
Dry cleaning = Nonflammable dry cleaning fluid. **Detergent** = mild detergent.

Remover	Water	Professional	Vacuum	Comments
				For washable clothing, soaking in warm water until the glue softens may be beneficial.
1				Consumers Union testers found that *Spray 'n Wash* stick laundry booster may help remove grass stains from washable fabrics.
				—
				—
				—
				—
	2			—
				—
				—
				For fresh stains on white washable cloth, you might want to try moistening a cloth with water, dipping it in baking soda and using it to blot the stained area.
2				It might be helpful to keep a box of individually packed alcohol wipes on hand at the office to help with removal of ballpoint pen ink.
		3		—
1				—
	3	4		Call 1-800-CRAYOLA for additional information.
		1		—

Ammonia. Vinegar. Enzyme = Enzyme-containing detergent. **Alcohol** = Rubbing alcohol. **Remover** = Nail polish or POG remover. **Water. Professiona**l = Call a professional. **Vacuum.**

Stain	Dry cleaning	Detergent	Ammonia	Vinegar	Enzyme	Alcohol	
Ink, stamp pad							
Ink, washable		1	2	3			
Iodine/ Merthiolate		2	3	4		1	
Jams and jellies		1	2	3	4		
Lacquer	2	3					
Lipstick/ lip gloss	2	3	4	5			
Margarine	1	2					
Mascara	2	3	4	5			
Mayonnaise	1	2	3				
Milk	5	1	2	3	4		
Mud		2					
Mustard		1	2	3	4		
Nail polish	2	3	4	5	6		
Newsprint	1	2					
Oil, automotive	1	2	3				
Oil, cooking	1	2	3				

Use the recommended cleaning agents in the order indicated in the table. For more information, see page 182.
Dry cleaning = Nonflammable dry cleaning fluid. **Detergent** = mild detergent.

Remover	Water	Professional	Vacuum	Comments
		1		—
				3% hydrogen peroxide may be helpful.
				—
				—
1				—
1				—
				—
1				—
				—
				—
		3	1	Allow to dry before vacuuming.
				Sunlight may quickly fade mustard stains.
1				—
		3		It might also help to first gently rub glycerine into the stain.
				Consumers Union testers found that *Spray 'n Wash* aerosol and *Shout* aerosol laundry boosters helped remove motor oil.
				—

Ammonia. Vinegar. Enzyme = Enzyme-containing detergent. **Alcohol** = Rubbing alcohol. **Remover** = Nail polish or POG remover. **Water. Professional** = Call a professional. **Vacuum.**

Stain	Dry cleaning	Detergent	Ammonia	Vinegar	Enzyme	Alcohol
Orange juice		1	2	3	4	
Paint, acrylic	2			3		
Paint, enamel	2	4				
Paint, finger		1	2	3		
Paint, oil-based	2	3	4			
Paint, water-based		1	2			
Peanut butter	1	2				
Pencil	1		3			
Perfume		1	2	3		
Perspiration	3		1	2		
Play-Doh	1	2				
Pudding		1	2	3	4	
Rust		2		1		

Use the recommended cleaning agents in the order indicated in the table. For more information, see page 182.
Dry cleaning = Nonflammable dry cleaning fluid. **Detergent** = mild detergent.

Remover	Water	Professional	Vacuum	Comments
				For washable clothing, pouring boiling water through the fabric from a height of 12 inches may help.
1 (POG)		4		—
1 (POG)	3	5		—
				—
1				—
				Although it may not be possible to remove dried latex paint, methanol (found in hardware stores) may help.
				—
	2			Use a clean eraser before attempting stain removal.
				—
				—
		3		—
				—
	3	4		For washable clothing, applying a paste of salt and vinegar, letting the garment stand for 30 minutes, and then washing may help. If this does not work, try using a paste of salt and lemon juice, followed by washing.

Ammonia. Vinegar. Enzyme = Enzyme-containing detergent. **Alcohol** = Rubbing alcohol. **Remover** = Nail polish or POG remover. **Water. Professional** = Call a professional. **Vacuum.**

Stain	Dry cleaning	Detergent	Ammonia	Vinegar	Enzyme	Alcohol	
Rubber cement	2	3					
Salad dressing	1	2					
Semen		1					
Shoe polish, paste	1	2	3	4			
Shortening	1	2					
Soft drinks		1	2	3			
Soot							
Sour cream	3	2					
Soy sauce		2	1				
Suntan lotion	1	2			3		
Syrup		1	2	3	4		
Tar, asphalt	2	3					
Tea	4	1		2	3		
Tomato sauce		1	2	3			
Unknown stains	5	1	2	3	4		

Use the recommended cleaning agents in the order indicated in the table. For more information, see page 182.
Dry cleaning = Nonflammable dry cleaning fluid. **Detergent** = mild detergent.

Remover	Water	Professional	Vacuum	Comments
1				—
				—
		2		—
		5		—
				—
				Use warm solutions on old stains.
		2	1	Masking tape can be substituted for vacuuming.
	1			For washables, a laundry booster may help.
		3		For washables, a laundry booster may help.
				For washables, a laundry booster and petroleum jelly may help.
				—
1 (POG)		4		—
				For washable clothing, pouring boiling water through the fabric from a height of 12 inches may help. Consumers Union testers also found that *Spray 'n Wash* stick laundry booster helped remove tea stains.
				—
				—

Ammonia. Vinegar. Enzyme = Enzyme-containing detergent. **Alcohol** = Rubbing alcohol. **Remover** = Nail polish or POG remover. **Water. Professional** = Call a professional. **Vacuum.**

Stain	Dry cleaning	Detergent	Ammonia	Vinegar	Enzyme	Alcohol
Urine (fresh)		1	2	3	4	
Urine (old)		1	3	2	4	
Vomit		3	2	1	4	
Water colors		1	2	3		
Water stains		1		2		
Wine		2	3	4		

Use the recommended cleaning agents in the order indicated in the table. For more information, see page 182.
Dry cleaning = Nonflammable dry cleaning fluid. **Detergent** = mild detergent.

Remover	Water	Professional	Vacuum	Comments
				—
				—
				—
	4			—
		3		3% hydrogen peroxide may help.
	1			In the restaurant, sprinkle fresh stains with club soda. For red wine spills, it might be beneficial to blot, sprinkle on white wine, and blot again. For washable clothing, pouring boiling water through the fabric from a height of 12 inches may help.

Ammonia. Vinegar. Enzyme = Enzyme-containing detergent. **Alcohol** = Rubbing alcohol. **Remover** = Nail polish or POG remover. **Water. Professional** = Call a professional. **Vacuum.**

Appendix C

Disposal of Household Cleaning Materials

The best way to dispose of a cleaning product is to use it up. If you can't use it, try to find someone who can—give it away. If either of these options is not feasible, check the label for recommendations regarding disposal. Some products may require special handling.

Water-soluble products. Water-soluble cleaning products are formulated to be treated in municipal sewage treatment plants or household septic systems. Accordingly, products that do not recommend special handling can be poured down the drain. This includes all-purpose cleaners, bleaches, dishwashing and laundry products, toilet bowl cleaners, and water-based metal cleaners and polishes. Be sure to run copious amounts of water while discarding, and never mix cleaning products—certain combinations may release dangerous fumes.

Solid cleaning products. Solid cleaning products—such as soap bars, rinse agents, soap pads, and towelettes—should be disposed of in the trash.

Solvent-based products. This category includes cleaning materials such as turpentine, mineral spirits, and other stuff used to clean paint brushes; spot removers; some metal and furniture cleaners; and any cleaning product labeled flammable. Solvent-based products should be disposed of in the same manner as household hazardous waste. Contact your municipality for local procedures, or call the manufacturer's telephone number—found on some product labels.

Do not flush solvent-based wastes down the toilet; do not pour them down a storm drain; do not dump them in a ditch, in your backyard, or in a vacant lot; and do not throw them out with the trash. If you store hazardous cleaning materials in anticipation of a collection day, keep them in well-ventilated racks, out of the reach of children and animals. Store them in the original container, tightly sealed, and kept dry. If a container begins to leak, place it in a larger intact container of similar material.

Household Hazardous Waste Collection Centers

Many municipalities have some type of household hazardous waste drop-off center. These services may be permanent or they may open periodically—several days per week, one or two days a year, or anything in between. Each center should list the specific types of waste it will and won't accept. Commonly, centers accept such items as drain cleaners, solvent-based cleaning products, paints, paint strippers, pesticides, batteries, gasoline, motor oil, charcoal lighter fluid, solvents, etc. Most do not accept banned chemicals such as PCBs, chlordane, and radioactive waste. Call your local sanitation authority for center locations and collection schedules.

Some communities may not accept empty containers from such products as bleach, toilet bowl cleaner, oven cleaner, and the like, either for recycling or regular trash collection. These containers may also have to go to the household hazardous waste collection site.

INDEX